Ask the Pool Guy's Everyday Guide to Swimming Pools

www.AskThePoolGuy.com

Ask the Pool Guy's Everyday Guide to Swimming Pools

Authors:

Allan Curtis, Sandi Maki

Reader's Responsibilities:

The authors, Al and Sandi, provide the information in this book to help pool owners understand and properly care for their swimming pools. All pools are unique, and all pool installations are too. Your own pool situation may be different than what's described here. ALWAYS refer to your manufacturer's instructions for questions on maintenance and repair. The authors are not responsible for any errors or omissions in this book and will not assume and disclaim any liability for any loss, damage or disruption to your own pool.

References to certain brands and equipment manufacturers are mentioned as helpful suggestions; we don't necessarily endorse any of those brands and/or information or their websites or other sources. It is up to you, the reader, to evaluate these suggestions for yourself. The authors are not for any damages that may arise out of the use of the information in this book.

(category: *advice, how-to*)

Happy Pools. Happy Customers. Happy Pool Guy.

This book is dedicated to pool owners everywhere...with special thanks to the Pool Guy's hard working team. We couldn't do this work without you. You all bring something special to our team, and we appreciate each one of you.

Preface

We love swimming pools. We love building them, servicing them, and keeping our pools and pool owners happy.

In this book you'll hear a little of our story, and a lot of our tips and thoughts on keeping your pool in great shape. Our goal for your pool is to have it running smoothly so you can enjoy it with family and friends, and make the memories that come with having a backyard pool.

We have put together some information to help you maximize your enjoyment, and answer many of the common pool service and maintenance questions. Several topics are also great troubleshooting guides and will serve as a valuable reference for you.

The most important section of this book is about Water Chemistry. Understanding your pool water chemistry is essential for your enjoyment, swimmer comfort and of the longevity of your pool surfaces, equipment and mechanicals.

The swimming pool season in Michigan, where *Ask the Pool Guy* was founded, typically runs from mid-April to mid-September. If you live in parts of the country where your season is longer, or even in the area where you don't winterize your pool, there is still plenty of information for you in this guide.

If you have any additional questions or problems, call our service hotline at 248-478-4978 or contact us via our website: www.AskThePoolGuy.com. We happily take calls and even pool design and build requests from around the country. We are prepared to help you troubleshoot, solve problems, and create the best swimming pool owner experience possible.

Happy Swimming!

Contents

Why Happiness Matters

{Al Curtis} Slogging through some prep work at a new build one day in March, I had one of those crystal clear moments. It was pouring rain – the kind of icy cold rain that felt like frozen needles on this "spring" day in Michigan – and I was aching and sore, standing up to my ankles in liquefied mud.

My body was screaming for mercy, having basically atrophied over the winter in this seasonal business I'm in, and I was soaked to the bone. The moment of clarity came when I realized – in spite of being wet, cold, hungry, sore and tired – I was whistling.

What I realized in that moment is that I was truly happy to be in this miserable pit of mud, because the vision in my head of what I was creating was far stronger than the physical discomfort I had to deal with in the moment.

That, my friends, is why happiness matters.

The Remarkable Energy of Happy

Interacting with customers and other contractors is great, and I cherish the relationships that I build. Still, for me there is a stronger sense of connection with water, with an experience, a true connection to creating an environment that people can experience happiness in.

Now, I grant you, if I just put in a pool, there will be some happiness created. Pools are a blast no matter who builds them.

My goal goes beyond that, to create this sense of space that honors the land and honors the people who will use it.

I truly believe in the law of attraction – like attracts like. Our bodies are made up primarily of water and are therefore attracted to water and if I can put the right energy into the water and do my very best to create a joyful space, then I am happy, the customers are happy – and I suspect that if we could look at the molecular level, that water is happy too!

Work Hard, Play Often

A key member of our crew is Penny, my adorable golden retriever. No matter what's going on, that silly dog makes me happy. You see, she serves as a constant reminder of the simple things in life and what's important – loyalty, friendship, and taking time to play.

Great example: I was digging a pool last month and she comes up to the excavator when I stop for a moment and she jumps up and drops her ball right in front of me. In other words, "Play with me. I don't care what you are doing, it doesn't matter what you are doing, and it's time to play."

I throw the ball, she runs and gets it, come backs and we do this several times and then she's good for a while. She constantly reminds me of the important of letting go of what we think is so important, and showing me that there's always time for joy.

It's moments like these that I'm left wondering why me? Why do I lead such a blessed life to be able to surround myself with such awesomeness?

I believe it comes down to a couple of key things. First is an awareness of how awesome life is, and how grateful I am to share it with terrific people – customers, crews, partners, and my fellow industry members. And secondly, and most importantly, letting that gratitude bubble up and fill me with joy.

Starting with Why

"Imagine a world where people wake up every day inspired to go to work, feel safe while they are there, and return home at the end of the day feeling fulfilled by the work they do, feeling that they have contributed to something greater than themselves."

{Sandi Maki} Let these words from Simon Sinek[i], author of the viral mega-hit book and motivational video *Start with Why*, sink in for a few moments.

Is this kind of world even within the realm of your imagination? Or are you, like so many others, cynical that we can find or create those kinds of workplaces and build those kinds of incredibly satisfying careers?

Is it possible to find fulfillment building pools and servicing pools?

For so many people, their work is simply something they must do, something that pays the bills. Sure, they may enjoy it. There may even be days when they could say they love it. Overall though, the weekend can't get here soon enough, right?

I used to feel this way about my work and the various jobs I held, until I discovered my own why.

I'm often asked—by customers, suppliers and other people in the industry—how I ended up as The Pool Girl, co-owner of Legendary Escapes, a swimming pool construction firm based in Michigan, and Ask the Pool Guy - Pool Service company with Al Curtis. Of all the possible careers open to me, why am I here?

It all started about a dozen years ago when I had the opportunity to join the pool company. At the time I was a single mom with two kids to support. The pool company offered a decent paycheck, flexibility when I needed it for the kids, and an opportunity to help grow a business from the inside out.

Saying yes was easy. The larger question is: Why have I stayed when I've had so many other choices over the years?

1

With a four-year college degree in Psychology and a solid background in marketing, there were any number of other ways I could spend my time that were a lot more glamorous than standing in mucky pool water or ankle deep in mud.

And while these opportunities paraded before me, there were times I was tempted. I stayed because the pool industry in general, and this company in particular, ultimately began to be the place where I could find the kind of fulfillment that only comes from living my own why.

I remember as a kid one of my all-time favorite books was *The Handy Girls Can Fix It* (Peggy Kahn, 1984). The book was about a group of girls who like to work with their hands and begin to offer their services doing painting, gardening and other odd jobs around the neighborhood. Eventually they help two younger kids in the neighborhood by creating a clubhouse for them, and discover how much fun it is to give back.

---

[1] Sandi's young kids at the start of her pool career

What has always stayed with me is the cool vibe of the clubhouse atmosphere; as I read that book again and again I could feel how awesome it must have been to be in that group, with everyone contributing their particular talents to make the end product the best it can be.

It makes perfect sense then that I fell in love with the pool business. Our company has always offered an encouraging, supportive environment, in which each person can contribute their own personal talents to the whole. Now that I am co-captain of this ship, I focus on this legacy and work hard to maintain and grow that atmosphere, from the front office to the field.

In the course of creating this company, we've also create a clubhouse for grownups. Al and I love surrounding ourselves with interesting things and interesting people, so it seemed like a natural extension of our work to open a clubhouse where business owners could share and contribute and enjoy hanging out.

Our "office" space has expanded over the years to include meeting rooms and lounge areas where our club members and friends can drop in, hang out, learn from each other and find support.

Through our Mastermind and marketing groups that we have created, we help small business owners discover their own why. We help them learn how to market their business using organic marketing principles that we applied to our pool company, teaching and sharing through examples and experience. In turn, they are able to apply the same principles and make it work for them.

Through our work with young people in the community, we see them discover their talents and grow as individuals, while they realize that we are all life-long learners regardless of our own educational backgrounds or pursuits.

2

Through our work with our team of pool crews and office staff, we take this same kind of supportive approach. Our team also happens to be predominantly women, both in the office and on the construction team. This is not because we set out to hire more women than men, it's because so many young women started to ask if they could work with us, and as it turns out they enjoy the work and do an outstanding job when they do. We are able to accomplish great things, with our very non-stereotypical construction crew.

Our entire team is included in discussions of our collective "Why". We also go over each individual's "Why" at our weekly team meetings, including the important question of their role on our team: "Does it make you happy?" The end goal for our workers is not to stay in the pool industry for ever—unless that's what they truly want to do, and in that case we'll support them in any way we can. Rather it's to empower them to find their own why, and find the courage to go seek that out in a big, bold way.

As I reflect again on Simon's words, I can imagine that kind of world, that kind of career. I've helped to create it, and I consider it a rare and beautiful privilege to go to work with these people every day.

---

[2] Our Pool Team

This book is in part a reflection of that joy.

New Pool Owner's Quick Start Guide

We have compiled this section as a quick at-a-glance way to get started with your swimming pool. If you collect the items on this list, and make sure you have them on hand, you'll be better prepared to take care of your pool. You will find more detailed info on specific topics further in the book.

Basic Supply ✓ List:

If you're new to the swimming pool world, you might be wondering what you'll need to get started with your pool. What chemicals should you have on hand? What equipment will you need? When you first walk into or click around in a pool store, it's easy to be overwhelmed by the amount of products you can choose. The list of things you'll need on a regular basis, though, is pretty manageable. Here's a basic list of supplies you should keep around. All of these items and their use is described in this book.

☐ *Phone Numbers:* The most important thing for you to have is the phone number to your local pool professionals, for service, chemicals, answers to your questions, and especially troubleshooting.

| |
| |
| |
| |
| |
| |

☐ *Vac (Vacuum) Head:* You'll use the vac head (attached to a pole and hose) to keep your pool clean and free of debris.

☐ *Vac Hose:* The vac hose attaches to the vac head and provides the suction needed to vacuum your swimming pool.

☐ *Pole:* The adjustable-length pole attaches to your vac head, brush, and leaf skimmer interchangeably. It is extendable to accommodate different pool depths and allow you to reach almost all areas of your pool without getting in.

☐ *Brush Head:* Attached to your pole, you brush the sides of your pool and keep them clean.

☐ *Leaf Skimmer:* The leaf skimmer attaches to the pole as well and allows you to skim leaves and debris (and bugs...gross!) from the surface of your pool.

☐ *Test Strips*/**Kit***:* Test strips will help you keep your water levels in check – they'll tell you the levels of chlorine, pH, and total alkalinity. This will let you know what chemicals you need to add to keep your pool clean, safe, and swimmable.

☐ *Stabilizer:* Stabilizer is a chemical that helps prevent chlorine dissipation due to sunlight. Intense sunlight can make it hard to maintain proper chlorine levels, so if your swimming pool is in direct sunlight you may need to use a stabilizer.

☐ *Alkalinity Plus:* Alkalinity+ raises the total alkalinity of your pool. Alkalinity that is too low can cause your pH levels to fluctuate excessively.

☐ *Calcium Hardness Increaser:* Calcium hardness increases water hardness to prevent surface etching, foaming, equipment corrosion, and scaling.

☐ *pH Plus:* pH+ raises the pH level of your pool water. The proper range (7.2-7.8) will allow your sanitizer to work more effectively, reduce equipment corrosion, reduce eye irritation, and reduce skin dryness.

☐ *pH Minus:* pH- lowers the pH of your pool water. It's important to keep your water in the proper pH range to optimize system performance, reduce corrosion, and reduce eye and skin irritation.

☐ *Algaecide:* algaecide controls and prevents all types of pool algae; a maintenance dose should be added weekly to the pool.

☐ *Water Clarifier:* You can use a clarifier or flocculant that will coagulate smaller particles together to be filtered out of the pool, or clumped together and settle to the bottom to be vacuumed out.

☐ *Ferrilron Tablet[ii]s:* If you have a sand filter, and are in an area with iron in your source water, these are a must have to sequester the iron out of your water to allow your sand filter to remove it.

What to Know About your Pool

Information to keep Handy

Here are the things you will need to know about your pool to have ready when talking to your pool company. Please make notes of any information you can find on your equipment such as model numbers, serial numbers, and sizes. This is helpful when looking into equipment issues and function.

Type of Pool Is the Pool an In-Ground or Above Ground Pool?
Construction What is the pool construction? Vinyl Liner - Gunite - Fiberglass - Hybrid Which Company Built the Pool?
Year Built When was the pool built?
Dimensions What are the dimensions of the pool? Length & Width

Depth

What are the Depths of the Pool?

Shallow End Depth:

Deep End Depth:

Water Volume

What is the volume of the pool in gallons?

Tile/Coping

How old is the liner or the tile/coping?

Winter Cover

What type of cover is used when winterizing the pool?

Safety Cover Manufacturer:

Year Cover was Installed:

Notes about the Equipment and Mechanicals:

Pump

Manufacturer:

Model:

Size (hp):

Size of Plumbing:

Age:

Year Installed/Replaced:

Filter Type Sand - DE - Cartridge

Manufacturer:

Model:

Size/Specs:

Age:

Year Installed/Replaced:

Last Cleaned/Serviced:

Type of Heater - Natural Gas - Propane - Electric - Heat Pump

Manufacturer:

Model:

Size (BTU):

Age:

Year Installed/Replaced:

Salt Generator

Manufacturer:

Model:

Size/Specs:

Age:

Year Installed/Replaced:

Automation System
Manufacturer:
Model:
Specs:
Age:
Year Installed/Replaced:
In-Floor Cleaning/Heating/Efficiency System
Manufacturer:
Model:
Specs:
Age:
Year Installed/Replaced:

Additional Notes:

Types of Swimming Pools

Fiberglass Pools

Fiberglass pools are one solid piece of fiberglass that can literally be 'dropped' in your backyard. Once the hole is dug, the pool is put into place, footed, plumbed, backfilled and the patio is poured.

Fiberglass pools come in many different shapes, colors, and finishes. There is some limitation to size, especially since they must be transported via truck to their final location.

Pros: Simple construction and installation in the proper methods for the climate where they are constructed.

Tips: Keep a fiberglass pool as full as possible at all times and maintain proper water chemistry to prolong the pool finish.

3

---

[3] Fiberglass Swimming Pool located in Michigan

Vinyl Liner Pools

Vinyl liner pools are constructed with a typical steel wall construction, footed into the ground, a hard bottom and finished with a vinyl liner insert.

They are constructed with wall panels, braces, steps, and a vinyl liner. All the components are assembled on site. The most popular materials for package pools are steel and polymer. These pools are engineered and designed in a factory environment then shipped to your home.

Pros: Easy to maintain, can be customized with different liner patterns, and repairs are usually quick and inexpensive.

Tips: Keep a vinyl liner pool as full as possible at all times and maintain proper water chemistry to prolong the life of the pool liner. The liner will need to be replaced eventually.

[4]

---

[4] Vinyl Liner Swimming Pool built by Legendary Escapes {RUS}

Gunite Pools

Gunite swimming pools are very common in commercial applications such as swim parks, hotels and schools/universities.

During construction the site is excavated, rebar is placed to shape the pool, the gunite material (mixture of cement and sand) is brought in and then poured/shot onto the rebar. The interior of the pool can be finished with tile, plaster, pebble, polished marble, or glass beads.

A product recently added to the market for gunite pool and fiberglass pool finish is: ecoFINISH[iii] is the manufacturer of aquaBRIGHT and polyFIBRO high performance *pool finishes*, a thermo-polymer finish solution.

Pros: High-end look when finished, flexible design options, and can be built in any desired shape.

Tips: Keep a gunite pool as full as possible at all times and maintain proper water chemistry to prolong the pool finish.

[5]

<hr>

[5] Gunite Swimming Pool built by Legendary Escapes {BEA}

Hybrid Swimming Pools

[6]I'm a true hybrid — a wild blend of pool guy, philosopher, social media geek/guru, entrepreneur and family man – so building hybrid pools is a perfect fit for me. With every project I undertake, I push the limits of creativity, applying best practice building techniques with new artistic expression. For me, hybrid pools offer unlimited opportunities to play and explore. And they've expanded my business in ways I've never dreamed possible.

I've been in the pool industry for almost my whole adult life, logging 28+ years in the business. Like you, I've seen new products, new trends and all sorts of innovations and I am always excited to learn something new that I can pass on to my customers and help create the perfect backyard lifestyle.

My adventure into "hybrid" pools began years ago when a customer wanted a traditional vinyl liner pool, but also wanted to put deck chairs in the shallow end and have a swim-up bar with stools that would sit in the water — possibly tearing the liner and causing expensive repairs.

---

[6] Hybrid Swimming Pool built by Legendary Escapes {RUS}

I suggested a combination of two traditional pool building techniques; the body of the pool would be done with a traditional vinyl liner, and the sun shelf plus swim-up bar and table area would be crafted in gunite. The clients absolutely loved the idea, and my career in hybrid pools was launched. With hybrid pools, I can challenge the boundaries of what my customers expect, and deliver a truly life-enhancing addition to their home.

Consumers are Driving Today's Trends

We get a lot of questions from pool owners—and from other pool companies—looking for more information on how we create our hybrid vinyl/gunite pools. For us, the process is a synergy; it's pieces from different types of projects, different types of pools, pulled together in new ways to create the optimal backyard environment.

The hybrid pools we create are in response to a growing trend: Customers are becoming more discerning and more specific all the time about what they want. It's no longer "keeping up with Joneses" and building what their neighbor has only bigger. Instead, we hear customers tell us how they want to use their outdoor space, what they want their lifestyle to be like, and it's these wishes that influence the design.

In building these more complex environments, it's not necessarily about discovering a brand new product or discovering something that didn't exist before and creating it. Rather, it's about taking what's already known to work and readily available, and appropriating it in a new way.

What I love about our work is the creativity of it all. Instead of saying "well, we've always done it this way" or having our customers pick a design out of book and plunking in the pieces, we like to say "what if..." What if we use the same products we are familiar with, but we use some of this over here, and blend in a little of that over there.

And that's what a hybrid pool is all about. It's taking all the benefits of vinyl–the comfort, the ease of use, the durability, the way it handles the water chemistry and stands up to the weather—and combining that with the durability and flexibility of custom gunite elements—the sun shelf that will hold lounge chairs, that hidden grotto or spill-over spa, and all those elements that require a different treatment than vinyl.

7

We've arrived at this hybrid place because we kept trying different ways of working with the existing products, and we realized that when we used everything that was available in a new way, magic happens. I mean real "wow, I had no idea our pool could look like this" kind of magic.

This kind of creative innovation is being driven by our customers, and their desire for something unique that truly expresses the kind of leisure life they are looking for. This kind of change—customer driven—means there is money in this industry for those of us willing to walk on the leading edge.

This leading edge is where I believe our industry needs to change. Pool design innovation has always been driven from the gunite side, because it's fabricated on site. Vinyl and fiberglass pools are more product driven, i.e. you pick your

---

7 Hybrid Swimming Pool Built by Legendary Escapes {BRN}

shape out of the product catalog, and we'll build that for you. Yes, we can do some design around that with some gunite features, but your basic shape is limited by the product.

That could change, and I believe the time is right for some of the leading vinyl designers to embrace this idea.

What I would love to see is designers in the vinyl liner industry come to the forefront. The well-known designers in our industry—the guys who have created incredible things and taken pools to the next level—are all gunite guys. Now there are some well-known vinyl names, sure, known for both the quality and quantity of their products, but we don't read much about these vinyl designers working on the front edge of custom pool design.

This is the road not traveled much at all...not reinventing the idea of a vinyl liner pool, but reimagining how it all goes together and offer vinyl liners that are custom-designed.

This idea, where we can use the existing benefits of vinyl in a bespoke way, is where we can blow the customers away.

If we look back to how the pool industry grew to where it is today, concrete pools were the original pools, then vinyl and fiberglass, but so many consumers still think that the only truly customizable options are in concrete. Our industry perpetuates that belief by keeping our design consultations product focused. To me that is the wrong approach.

Instead, we need to ask the deeper questions up front about what they expect out of their pool environment, and then design an environment to meet that request. There is a tremendous amount of design work that can be done in vinyl. We work with some terrific vinyl providers who provide the customization that we need, using standard panels that are put together in non-standard ways, repurposing instead of reinventing.

Right now I believe there is a huge opportunity for these designers to step up and showcase what they can do instead of offering the "pick one" approach.

The hybrid pool is more than a trend; this is happening as a result of customer demand and a changing market. The vinyl industry leaders are not necessarily addressing it fully...but they will. They'll follow the money, like all industries.

Instead of following the money, why not try leading the pack? What if we ask ourselves what more could we do for our customers? Be an early adopter, living on the front edge of that bell curve where all the innovation happens, not the long tail. Yes, you're taking risks...but isn't staying where you are and being a follower a bigger risk?

The customer is driving change in our industry, insisting on more custom solutions and less "out of the box" thinking. We will either be pushed in that direction, or we can innovate and bring it to the customer. This is where the vinyl designer industry has a huge opportunity.

Sure it requires more time up front on the design end, but the finished product—and the customer relationship—will be a hundred times better for it.

Ceramic Tile in a Vinyl Liner Pool

We use TRU-Tile, TruTile/Ceramic Tile Mount combines the beauty of tile with the low maintenance of a vinyl liner, a track

Tru-Tile Vinyl Liner Installation

system from Latham Industries that allows us to add ceramic tile with a vinyl liner in our pools.

Maintenance on this system means the tile can be cleaned like a traditional ceramic surround in a gunite pool, with care taken not to scratch or dislodge the liner from the track.

If you are a homeowner with a Tru-Tile system, and you ever experience issues, please call for service from your pool professional. If you don't know who services Latham's Tru-Tile in your area, please contact Latham Pool[iv] directly.

Ceramic Tile with Vinyl Liner

Gunite Swimming Pool Finishes

When installing or renovating a gunite swimming pool there are several options for the type of finish available.

A gunite pool is sometimes also referred to as a concrete pool, shotcrete pool, or marcite pool.

Shotcrete is concrete (or sometimes mortar) conveyed through a hose and pneumatically projected at high velocity onto a surface, as a construction technique.

Shotcrete is usually an all-inclusive term that can be used for both wet-mix and dry-mix versions. In the pool construction trade however, the term "shotcrete" refers to wet-mix and "gunite" refers to dry-mix; in this context, these two terms are not interchangeable. Marcite is a type of pool finish, also referred to as white plaster, as well as pebble, colored plaster, quartz, polished surface or glass bead finishes.

8

---

8 Gunite Pool Under Construction by Legendary Escapes {DRA}

Gunite Swimming Pool Surface Finishes

The pool surface can be finished with the traditional white marcite, the marcite could be dyed a color, or a pebble or other aggregate finish could be used.

Cleaning of the pool surface can typically be done with a solution of muriatic acid and water, or liquid chlorine will also work on some organic staining on the pool surface.

An acid wash uses muriatic acid and water, with scrubbing and a wire bristle brush to etch the top surface layer of the pool off to release surface stains. Care should be taken during an acid wash to keep the pool from experiencing hydrostatic pressure (water pressure issues). It is also important not to acid wash a pool too often, as a finish can only handle so much of this type of cleaning.

NOTE: If a gunite pool is ever painted, acid washing is not advised unless the manufacturer's directions call for it specifically. Also, once a gunite pool is painted, you may need to re-paint the pool often, as it is not often a long lasting solution.

Pool Finish Types:

> ➤ Marcite - White or Blue
> ➤ Pebble - A variety of colors and pebble sizes
> ➤ Quartz - Exposed Aggregate
> ➤ Tile
> ➤ ecoFinish - thermoplastic resin
> ➤ Paint

Common Swimming Pool Patio Types

The most common types of patio for a swimming pool include:

- ➤ Concrete – broom finished
- ➤ Exposed Aggregate
- ➤ Stamped
- ➤ Colored/Textured* (Clearly, our favorite)
- ➤ Tile (indoor use)
- ➤ Brick Pavers

Broom Finished

[9]Broom Finished Concrete is sometimes the most economical option. It includes using basic concrete, in its lightest base color, and finishing with a broom for a relatively smooth surface (without polishing). A polished concrete pool deck would simply be way too slippery. The drawback of this style pool deck is that it looks very plain and basic, and if you have

---

[9] Vinyl Liner Pool with Broom Finished Concrete

spent time and energy investing in a creative and artistic pool, this style patio will not necessarily offer a finishing touch. This style concrete also dates a pool. It was commonly used in the 70's, 80's and 90's to put a 4' walkway around three sides of the pool, with some extra for a table and chairs. The pool in the photo above was built in the late 80's, and had a recent liner replacement done.

Pretty = No, Slippery = No, Comfortable = Yes

[10]Exposed Aggregate

Exposed Aggregate Patios are certainly eye catching and beautiful. The drawback around a swimming pool is that you hardly dare to walk on it barefoot. The exposed aggregate, while it looks pretty also offers areas to stub your toe, and a rough, uneven surface for walking on. To get the shiny look that is often seen in this type of patio, the surface can also become slick when wet due to the sealant used on the patio.

---

[10] Hybrid Swimming Pool by Legendary Escapes with Exposed Aggregate Patio

Remember as well, the darker the color, the warmer or hotter the patio will be to the touch – and bare feet are sensitive. Pretty = Yes, Slippery = Often, Comfortable = Maybe not so much.

Stamped Concrete Patio

11

Stamped Concrete Patio is also a pretty option. Many people like the stamped shapes that make the pool look like it has a stone pattern in the surround. Traditional stamped patios offer a universal design in the concrete finish. They are usually finished with a sleek sealant to pull the color into the stamp design and leave them looking glossy. This will usually result in a patio that is warmer to the touch, and extremely slippery when wet. We do anticipate the area around the pool getting wet with swimmers and pool side activity. Pretty = Yes, Slippery = YES!

---

[11] Gunite Swimming Pool in Michigan

Textured Concrete Patio

[12]Textured Concrete Patio is clearly the Pool Guy's favorite application for a swimming pool surround. It offers a nice textured finish that is a great design element, as well as easy to walk on with bare feet. The natural texture lines also allow for some disguise of the results of pouring concrete in Michigan. With our freeze/thaw cycle it is likely that cement will at some point in its life crack, and the natural texturing of the patio allows the cracks to be somewhat hidden and blend into the environment. We've found that the textured patios with slight color variations offer a good experience for bare feet in terms of warmth, ease of walking on, and texture to prevent slipping. Textured patios can be sealed to keep in the color, using a seal that penetrates into the concrete rather than forming a glossy layer on top.

Pretty = yes, Slippery = no, Comfort for bare feet = good!

---

[12] Vinyl Liner Pool with Custom Waterfall built by Legendary Escapes

Tiled Patio

[13]Tiled Swimming Pool Surrounds are most often used in indoor application where regular cleaning is needed. They are typically more slippery when wet than a concrete finish which is why there is no running around the pool! It is not recommended to tile the surround of an outdoor pool, especially in Michigan, where weather and other elements would be too much for the tile to handle.

Pretty = yes, Slippery = yes

Brick Paver Patio

Brick Pavers around pools in Michigan are not such a good idea. Brick pavers look lovely. They often create geometric patterns and designs that are eye catching and nice to look at. The problem with brick pavers surrounding a pool in Michigan are that we have more water, and groundwater to deal with than pools in other climates. When a pool is installed in Michigan, whether it is gunite, or vinyl, or fiberglass (Which has its own set of challenges), the patio is typically poured up to the edge of the pool or the coping.

There is typically and expansion line left in between the coping and patio to allow for some ground movement, and then this line is filled with self leveling joint compound to prevent water

---

[13] Gunite Indoor Swimming pool built by Legendary Escapes

from getting in between the patio and the pool. When brick pavers are used, there is no prevention of water from getting between the patio and the pool, and all of that water can float vinyl liners, and it can cause ground water pressure to become high surrounding a gunite or fiberglass pool. We have seen too many instances of a fiberglass pool popping out of the ground, cracking and shifting when there are contributing factors to instability. If you have the option to choose anything but brick pavers around your pool in Michigan, please do. You may be fine in the long run, but if you are not, it will be a very expensive issue to fix.

14

Keep in mind when choosing your pool patio style that the darker the colors in the patio, the warmer the patio will be.

It's a great idea to visit some patio styles and determine what your options are before making your choice. You will also want to take off your shoes and do the touch test to see if it works for you. We often have customers do this while choosing colors

---

14 Brick Paver Patio around a Firepit at a Legendary Escape

and styles of pool coping as well. It may look pretty, but if you can't walk on it or sit comfortably dangling your feet into the pool, it may not be the best choice for your pool.

Caring for your Pool - An Owners Guide

In this section we'll talk about how to care for you pool...from season opening to close, and what needs to be done each day, week and month throughout the season.

Opening Your Swimming Pool

Opening your swimming pool in the spring is a very exciting time! In southern climates pools are often left open, but aren't used and are left dormant or with minimal attention.

The Steps for a pool opening typically include:

- ✓ Remove the Pool Cover
- ✓ Install Deck Equipment
- ✓ Add Water - by Hose or Water Truck
- ✓ Prep Equipment for Running
- ✓ Prime the Pump, Start the Heater
- ✓ Clean the Pool, Brush and Vacuum
- ✓ Water Chemistry Check, Shock
- ✓ Add Chemicals and Salt
- ✓ Start Your Filtration System & Vacuum
- ✓ Jump in!

15

---

[15] Anna enjoys her Legendary Escapes Hybrid Swimming Pool!

Here is a much more detailed description of these steps:

Step 1. Remove Your Pool Cover

A solid winter cover, such as a plastic cover with water bags or an automatic cover will need to be drained of water. This can be done with a cover pump, or a pool team will typically have a large pump with 2-3" hoses to quickly remove the water.

Be certain to check your pool cover, a hole or loose weave in your cover can cause you to pump water out of the pool itself, resulting in a water level that gets too low.

[16]This can be a serious issue for fiberglass or gunite pool owners, so please monitor your pool as you drain the water! See the photo on the right. This is called a pop-out and it's a major repair.

The combination of brick pavers around this pool, as well as pumping too much water out of the pool may have contributed to this pop-out issue.

---

[16] A fiberglass pool pop out situation.

Automatic Covers

Your automatic cover should have a cover pump which is left on the pool all the time when the cover is closed. This should be functioning to remove the water from the pool cover as needed. It may freeze during the coldest part of winter, and resume operation in the spring. It is often a great idea to add water under your pool cover before the team arrives to open your pool with an automatic cover. It will allow the cover to move freely over the pool with less strain on the cover, and it will allow the pool team to vacuum and clean your pool when the water is at a level that will allow the pool to fully function.

17

---

[17] A Hybrid Swimming Pool built by Legendary Escapes with a Coverstar Automatic Cover

Pool Opening in Progress

[18]Our opening crew opened this vinyl liner pool, and while we could describe it to you, perhaps a photo series is worth even more.

Step 1: Wow, this is going to be fun! Notice the swimming pool, plastic cover, water-bags, and leaves buried in the murky water.

The Crew used a large trash pump with 3" hoses to remove the water from the top of the cover, while scooping leaves off the top.

Progress! We've gotten the water and the leaves off the cover, now we can remove the water-bags and carefully pull the cover off the pool.

While water is being added to the pool to bring it back up to operational level, the crew vacuums the pool with an external vacuum to get fine debris and leaves off the bottom. This helps [19]immensely with water clarity and sets you up for an enjoyable spring.

---

[18] Vinyl liner swimming pool with plastic cover, waterbags and dirty water
[19] The cover is off and the crew is using an external vacuum

Step 2. Install Deck Equipment

The equipment that was removed during the closing will be reinstalled, such as the hand rail and ladders.

Make sure ladders that go back in pools, especially vinyl liner or fiberglass, have ladder bumpers on them so they don't scratch or puncture the pool's surface.

20

21

---

[20] Ladder, note the white ladder bumper caps. These must be present to protect the liner

Step 3. Add Water - By Hose or Water Truck

The cover is off, there is a bit of murky water under the cover, this could be due to small holes in the cover allowing water through. It's good to get a new cover when this happens.

If your pool cover is plastic or an automatic cover, you may refill the pool with a hose, or a water truck. A water truck may be chosen because it is a quick way to top off the pool, or in cases of poor source water, high in iron content etc. Your pool team should be able to help you determine the best option for your situation.

22

Add enough fresh water to bring your swimming pool to the desired height which is typically about ¾ of the way full, in your skimmer. This allows debris to pass into the skimmer and

---

21 Hybrid Swimming Pool by Legendary Escapes
22 Filling a Hybrid Swimming Pool by Legendary Escapes with a Garden Hose

allows enough water to flow through so your system doesn't get any air infused during full operation. This is too low and the debris can't get into the skimmer.

23

Fill Water for your Swimming Pool

When it comes to your swimming pool, water is the most important component. Having beautiful clear water isn't as difficult as it sounds, but the quality of your pool water starts the moment you begin filling it.

There are many ways to fill up a swimming pool.

---

23 The water should be half way up the skimmer, to 3/4 the way up at all times for proper operation

24

If you have good water pressure out of the garden hose, that is the most common way to fill your pool. City dwellers may run into water fees for both the filling and disposal of water if your water is metered. In this case, sometimes a homeowner will opt to hire a water truck.

If your water comes from a well, if your well can handle the volume of water you will need to fill a pool, you can fill it that way. In some areas of the country the source water may be very poor quality for a swimming pool fill and have minerals that will cause discoloration to the water, and staining to the pool and surfaces. In this case you will want to decide if you would like to treat the water to remove these substances, or if you'd like to hire a water truck as well.

---

24 Penny enjoys the water from the water truck as the Pool Guy and Erin look on

25

Well water high in iron on the left, treated with Ferrites on the right, 24 hour time lapse

Some homeowners are tempted to find alternative sources of water such as pumping it in from a lake or pond (not a great idea, this may be very cloudy water and very difficult to balance with all the organic matter typically found in lakes and streams.

We've had the occasional homeowner who thought they'd save money by tapping into a fire hydrant (this ends up being much more costly than you'd imagine, even with permission of the city). Some cities and municipalities have clean water in the fire hydrant system, however more often the water quality is not advisable for using in a swimming pool. Filling a swimming pool from fire hydrant water can create more problems with water balance and can take days or weeks to fix.

---

25 Before and After FerriTab treatment in a vinyl liner pool with a sand filter, 24 hour time lapse

Water Trucks

A pool under construction often looks much bigger or smaller than when it is full of water depending on your perspective. It's always interesting to see just how much goes in there!

[26]If you hire a water truck to fill your pool, when it is newly installed or during your season opening, you will also have an idea how much water is in your pool.

Trucks vary in the load they carry, ranging from small loads of about 5,000 gallons per truck, to some of the larger residential trucks carrying 12,000 gallons of water. When we do a vinyl liner replacement or a gunite renovation, typically we ask the homeowner to bring in a truck load or two, or sometimes three, of water to get the pool full quickly. It can take a long time with a garden hose. Especially in instances where water quality is an issue, in areas of high iron or other mineral content, having water brought in by truck is also an excellent idea.

Water Truck Sizes

If you need water quickly during a pool renovation, or during new construction, a water truck will be your best option. Water trucks vary in size, and many will do partial or full loads of water, depending on how much you need. The average water truck we hire here in Michigan can carry 5,000-12,000 gallons of water.

---

[26] Vinyl liner pool under construction by Legendary Escapes

27

This water is clean, clear, and generally of great quality. Water trucks often use water filling stations that are available in many municipalities for delivering good quality water.

During your swimming pool opening if you have any doubts or concerns about using your garden hose, or the depth of your well, please consider a truck. One truck of water should be sufficient to top off most residential swimming pools.

If you are having your liner replaced, your gunite acid washed, or need to fill your pool completely for another reason, most swimming pools will take 1-2 truck loads. In most cases, it's perfectly okay to top off your swimming pool with hose water or another water source. It is important to start with the majority of your pool water being clean, clear, and high quality.

---

27 Ken with BlueWater Trucking, Michigan delivers water for a pool fill

28

If you start with clean water, you have a much better foundation to build your water chemistry and keep your water clarity. This means a much more enjoyable swim season for you, and a pool and equipment that can function at their best capacity.

---

28 Filling a vinyl liner pool after replacing the vinyl liner

Step 4. Prep Equipment Pad

Before you start up your swimming pool pump and filter system, be sure that all lines are open. Make sure the pump and skimmer baskets are in place and free from debris. Remove any plugs or gizzmos from the skimmer that were added during the closing.

Check your pump basket for your plugs and gauges. This is where they are commonly stored over the winter.

[29][30]The valve on the left is open. The one on the right is closed.

[29] Swimming Pool Eqiupment System
[30] The valve on the left is open, on the right is closed

Step 5. Prime the Pump, Start the Heater

Follow your manufacturer's guidelines for starting up your pool heater, pool filter, and pump. Make sure to start each new season with a clean filter.

31

---

[31] Swimming pool equipment system, two skimmers, main drains, sand filter, salt generating system, pool heater (all by Pentair)

Step 6. Clean the Pool, Brush and Vacuum

Remove leaves, twigs, and other large debris from the pool's bottom using a leaf rake. If you cannot see the pool bottom it is important that you do this repeatedly to get as much debris from the pool bottom as possible. If the water is too murky and you can't see the bottom there may be too much debris on the drains that may prevent the pool system from operating properly. It can also suck in too much debris and clog your pump impeller and filter.

32

A large amount of debris can also increase your chlorine demand. A pool that is cloudy but free of debris will be easier for the filtration system to handle.

---

32 Vacuuming during a pool opening with algae coating the vinyl liner

Step 7. Water Chemistry Testing

33

Once you open and fill your pool it will most likely need to be shocked. You will also need to test your water within about a week so you can balance the chemicals. We suggest a set of test strips[34] or the computerized option by AquaChek[v].

It is a great idea to keep a record of your pool water chemistry. It serves as a helpful tool for diagnosing any issues that may come up. If more than one person services your pool it will also help everyone to know what has been done.

---

[33] Sample water test strip, AquaChek
[34] We suggest AquaChek's test strips

Step 8. Add Chemicals and Salt

Once you test your water, begin adjusting your pool water chemistry. Take note of the water chemistry section in this book to understand what each chemical is, and what order you should add chemicals.

If you have a salt water pool/chlorine generator you will likely have to add salt to the pool when you open it. Please note that your salt generator may not begin to make chlorine until the pool reaches a certain temperature, so you will need to use an alternative method with cold water. Refer to your manufacturer's directions for clear instructions on this.

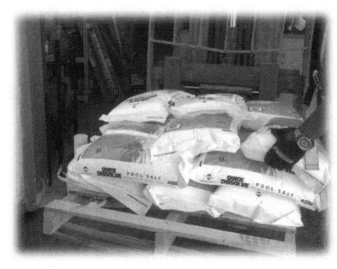

35

If you do need to add salt, make sure to add one or two bags at a time and allow plenty of time for the water to circulate. It's much easier to add a bit more than adjust if you add too much and the balance swings the other way.

---

35 A pallet of pool salt ready for pickup

36

Once the pool is full and at normal operating level you can prime the pump and start the filter.

Typically the filter is backwashed (by our team) during the pool closing, so additional backwashing is not needed. If you are not sure if this was done on your pool, a little extra backwash cycle won't hurt.

Once the water is at the appropriate level for the skimmer to function, slowly open the skimmer valve to bleed the air out of the line and get back to normal function. At this point you can also hook up your vacuum (refer to the vacuuming section in the book for step by step instructions, or head to YouTube and look for the @askthepoolguy[vi] tutorial on vacuuming).

---

[36] Salt on the edge of the pool ready for addition

[37]You may want to manually vacuum the pool the first time in the spring (or have your pool team do this for you) even if you have a handy dandy automatic pool cleaner. (Note: most automatic cleaners work best in pool water that is over 55 degrees).

---

[37] Vacuuming a pool through the skimmer during a gunite pool opening

38

Brush down the walls to loosen any debris at the waterline, and to allow the chemicals to reach all areas of the pool and do their work. Make sure you have large debris out of the pool, no shortcuts here, to protect your automatic cleaner from any excessive debris and trauma!

Shocking the pool is typically done by adding one pound of shock per 10,000 gallons of water. In areas where liquid chlorine is available, we recommend that as a fast acting option that is safe for all types of swimming pools. If you have a salt water/chlorine generating pool you can also use chlorine to shock your pool. If you do need to add  granular shock to your pool, mix it in a bucket with water before adding to the perimeter of your pool. Brushing after you add the shock is a great idea just in case any settles.

When in doubt, follow label directions for the proper instructions to shock your pool.

Be careful, especially if you have a vinyl liner or hybrid pool(TM) not to allow granular shock to land on your liner. It can sink to

---

the bottom and if it sits can cause bleaching, or discoloration of your liner.

39

Step 9. Jump IN!

40

Once you are all set, you can jump in! People often ask how long they need to wait after the opening to swim. You can jump

---

39 Rick vacuums a vinyl liner pool during a pool opening
40 Erin and Casey give this pool a thumbs up! {Filling during the initial startup of the Hybrid Swimming Pool built by Legendary Escapes}

in as soon as you'd like, just allow the shock that is added to the pool to disperse and do their job a bit before you do. If you do jump in too quickly make sure to shower after using the pool to rinse off any excess chemicals.

Look for New Technology

Each year is a great time to reassess your pool and pool equipment. Now may be the time for you to look into a salt system, an automatic pool cleaner like a Dolphin, or even look into weekly service for your pool.

41

Look to your local swimming pool service company for assistance, many, including Ask the Pool Guy will offer a new user training for the cost of a service call. This allows you to learn your pool system, and it allows our team to get to know your pool to better service you during the pool season.

Swimming Pool Automation

---

41 EasyTouch Automation by Pentair

The Pool Guy's favorite automation system is the EasyTouch®[vii] system that works with the Pentair equipment. You will find this system on all of our new swimming pool projects – either the pool only or the pool and spa combo.

The best way to learn your new automation system is to get into the programming menus and see what happens when you start to schedule and push buttons.

iPhone/Android Control with ScreenLogic®[viii]

There are a couple of ways to put a remote on your pool. The best would be to add the screen logic system that works with your Pentair panel. Then you can download the Phone/iPad/Android app or control it from your home computer. To install we would need to put a box in at your home computer (or at your router) and run a cable out to the pool control panel, and install the Screen Logic system there.

Pool Care Through the Season

Care of your Pool

When a new gunite pool is installed no matter the finish of marcite, plaster, pebble or quartz, the finish needs to cure during the first several weeks. It is suggested that salt be added after the first month of use, though water chemistry should be balanced immediately.

With any pool finish, clear and sparkling water doesn't necessarily mean balanced water, and it is important to begin checking your chemical levels every few days at the beginning and then at least weekly with test strips after that.

A regular maintenance schedule should be followed to keep the pool clean, and your water chemistry balanced. At first pool maintenance has a lot of unfamiliar terms and may seem complicated. Stick with it though, it will become simple and quick the more you know.

42

---

42 Vinyl Liner Swimming Pool built by Legendary Escapes

Care for Cleaning Equipment and Accessories

Store your pool chemicals and equipment out of the sun, and in a place that will preserve their life span. Liquid chlorine especially should be stored away from elements as its gas can become corrosive if stored indoors, however it also needs to be kept out of the sun which will shorten its lifespan.

Carry your vac hose versus dragging it to prevent snags and punctures. When it is not in use, drain and roll up the hose, and store it out of the sun. Don't overload your leaf skimmer while using so it doesn't bend, break or tear.

43

Basic Maintenance Schedule

Your maintenance needs will vary for your pool. The amount of maintenance needed can change with your swimmer load, with the climate of your region, and of the seasonal weather and temperatures you encounter. Because of this, there is not a one size fits all maintenance schedule, you will need to determine the needs of your pool. There are some universal maintenance

---

43 Hybrid Swimming Pool/Spa built by Legendary Escapes

recommendations you can consider when developing your schedule.

Remember that prevention, especially with water chemistry monitoring will help ensure your pool stays clear, and you protect the pool and equipment.

The maintenance you should begin with your pool are listed here:

Test Your Water - this should be done at least once a week with a home tester - it can be done as often as every couple of days. We also recommend taking a water sample into your local pool store once per month for an accurate computer test.

Chemical Additions - read the label directions on your chemicals if your test indicates you need any. You will want to add chemicals after you have backwashed the pool (if needed) so you don't just put chemicals down the drain. Also take care to add only one chemical at a time as they may react with each other. Also follow a routine of adjusting the alkalinity before pH, and pH before altering the stabilizer and calcium.

Use your pool net to skim leaves and remove debris from your pool.

Use your brush to remove dirt, and algae from the pool walls and floor. If you have iron staining, a common issue with well water, add a product that is ascorbic acid based to release the stain from the pool surface, and then brush. Make sure to use a metal remover after this so the stain will not return.

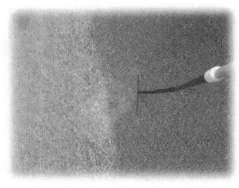

44

Clean and empty all baskets - in your skimmer(s) and the pump.

Vacuum - be sure to use the correct vacuum for your pool, and remove any settled dirt or leaves from the pool. Watch the pump basket and your filter pressure during this process. Often you will need to perform a backwash with a sand or de filter when the vacuuming process introduces a large amount of debris to the filter system. In cases of severe debris and algae, you may need to use the waste feature to remove the water from the pool and bypass the filter, rather than forcing the water through the filter system.

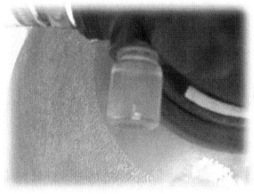

45

---

[44] Brushing a bleached spot on a vinyl liner pool to assess the damage
[45] The sight glass on a sand filter

Clean your filter - if you have a sand filter or a DE filter, cleaning = backwashing the filter, followed by a rinse.

46

if it is a cartridge filter, then rinse the individual pleated filter elements with a garden hose and a pressurized nozzle (Note: too much pressure on the filter cartridge material may tear it).

Your DE filter should be thoroughly cleaned once a season, and checked over for tears or rips.

---

46 Backwash hose with dirty/iron content water

47

Shock your pool regularly, even with a salt system. You need to shock to reach break-point chlorination to keep your pool sanitizing system functioning as it should.

Once you get to know your pool you can develop your own maintenance schedule. The number of swimmers, your climate and seasonal temperatures and precipitation will all be factors in the amount of care and maintenance your pool needs. Remember, even if your water looks clear, it doesn't mean your water is balanced. Improper water chemistry is one of the leading causes of problems with pools and pool equipment.

48

---

47 Algae covered DE filter grids out for a soak and cleaning
48 A friendly pool visitor, who often adds complications to pool cleaning

Daily Maintenance

Pool Water Chemistry

Maintaining your water chemistry is critical for your swimming pool. Daily (or at the very least weekly) chemical testing is essential for your pool and equipment to be protected from improper chemical levels. Instructions for testing are included with test kits, we recommend a 5 in 1 or 7 in 1 test strip which is a quick and easy way to get a reading of your water chemistry levels.

Proper water chemistry can prevent scaling (scale forming on your pool surface and equipment). It can also prevent etching of pool surfaces, as well as the growth of algae (which may present as a slimy feeling before you notice any color to it).

You will need to pay attention to all of your chemicals, not just chlorine and pH.

Find a good pool store in your area where you can bring in a water sample once a month for a computerized test of your chemicals and recommendations beyond your regular at home water testing.

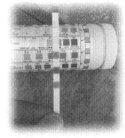
49

---

[49] AquaCheck Sample Test Strip

Weekly Maintenance

Your pool should be brushed down once a week, especially during hot weather. Take time to brush the water line, and the sides and bottom of the pool. Vacuum the pool when you see debris with your manual vacuum or by using an automatic pool cleaner. The benefit of an automatic pool cleaner such as the Dolphin is that the walls and floor are continually scrubbed, eliminating the need for much of your manual brushing and pool maintenance.

Weekly Pool Cleaning and Service

Weekly pool service should be performed on your pool. You can take care of it, or you can join a weekly cleaning service route so someone else can take care of it for you.

Here are some common weekly service tasks:

- ✓ Chemical Balance Analysis
- ✓ Chemical Adjustment
- ✓ Chemical Delivery to Replenish your Supply (you supply all chemicals for sanitizing i.e. chlorine, salt)
- ✓ Pool Equipment Checkup
- ✓ Skim Surface
- ✓ Brush Tiles *
- ✓ Vacuum *
- ✓ Empty skimmers
- ✓ Empty pump basket
- ✓ Empty pool cleaner bag/basket
- ✓ Backwash filter*

Even with a weekly pool service agreement, you as the pool owner will still need to keep an eye on the pool in between visits. You never know when something will blow into the pool, clog your baskets or surge in electricity. It's best to know at least the basics about your system so you can perform some of the tasks.

Weekly Service Log

Date:

Weather: Temperature Readings:

☐ Sunny   Air
☐ Overcast   _____
☐ Windy   Pool
☐ Rainy   _____
                                 Spa
                                 _____

Services Completed:

☐ Surface Skimmed
☐ Waterline Scrubbed
☐ Vacuumed
☐ Auto Cleaner Serviced
☐ Baskets Cleaned
☐ Pump Basket Cleaned
☐ Sanitizer Added
☐ Filter Cleaned
☐ Filter Pressure ____

☐ Water Analysis   Target Range
   ☐ Chlorine   ____   1.0-2.0ppm
   ☐ pH   ____   7.4-7.6
   ☐ Alkalinity   ____   80-100ppm
   ☐ Calcium   ____   200-300ppm
   ☐ Stabilizer   ____   40-60ppm
   ☐ Salt   ____   2800-3500ppm

Chemicals Applied

Skimming Your Pool Surface

Pool Nets

There are several styles of pool nets available on the market. There are a few options you will want to have on hand.

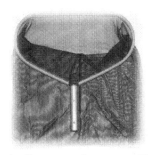

[50]The leaf rake has a wide opening and a deep net, great for scooping debris and leaves from the pool bottom. This style of net can also be used to skim leaves off the surface of the pool, however the skim net may be easier to maneuver for this task.

[51]The skim net or skimmer net is shallow, and is usually a frame with netting across it to make for easy skimming of the pool surface to remove leaves, lawn clippings insects and debris that are floating on the surface of the water.

Leave and debris should be removed from your pool to prevent collecting or clogging on the main drains, which will restrict water flow and circulation. They can also clog your skimmer baskets, another common reason water flow and circulation will be reduced. Leaves and debris can increase your chlorine demand, and not allow it to keep up with other contaminants in your water, and allow the growth of algae. Excessive leaves will also clog vacuum equipment, and if left settled long enough can stain and leave tannin stains on the pool surface.

Netting can be a quick and easy task, do it anytime you notice leaves or debris present. It may be especially needed after a

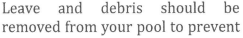

[50] Leaf and Debris Net
[51] Surface Skimming Net

wind or rain storm, or during the fall season if you have a lot of trees and landscaping near your pool.

Clean your Skimmer Baskets

[52]When your pool water flow slows down, this will be indicated on your pressure gauge on the filter. You may also notice your pool water seems to be circulating more slowly. The first thing to check when your water circulation is poor is your skimmer basket to be sure that 1) the water level is high enough for proper function and 2) that leaves and debris are not clogging the flow.

The water level in the skimmer should be at least 1/2 to 3/4 up the skimmer opening, just enough for debris to flow under the top lip of the skimmer to collect in the skimmer basket, but not too high that the debris can't get in.

Depending on how high your skimmer is installed on your pool wall, as all skimmers may be set a little differently will determine the water level for your pool. Another variable will be the size of your plumbing and your pump speed. You want to have enough water in your pool to draw a constant flow of water without causing air to enter the filtration system, or the whirlpool effect in your filter which can also add air into your system.

Depending on the size of your pool you may have one or more skimmers.

To perform maintenance on your skimmer:

---

[52] Vinyl Liner Pool and Skimmer at Proper Fill Level

- ✓ Remove the skimmer lid from the pool deck. Remove the skimmer basket from the opening. If your basket is full of leaves you may need to turn off your pump to release the suction pulling the basket down.
- ✓ Handles on pool skimmers sometime break, and there are often after market skimmer basket options with larger handles available. If your skimmer basket becomes broken, or is difficult to remove, you may want t look into basket alternative.
- ✓ Empty the contents of your skimmer (far enough away from your pool that it won't just blow back in). Be careful not to chip or break your skimmer basket during this process.
- ✓ You may also clean the basket with a garden hose, or a quick tip from our service team is to grab a bucket and scoop some water from the pool, insert the skimmer basket (this also works for your pump basket) and give it a good swish and swirl upside down. This should release the debris and give you a clean basket to reinsert.
- ✓ Return the skimmer and replace your lid.

During this process, make sure your skimmer basket seats in the skimmer properly. Especially in gunite pools a common skimmer basket with the floating top can get stuck in various positions and affect the skimmer operation, and in many cases if stuck long enough can cause the whirlpool phenomenon and affect your pump function.

Notes:

- ✓ [53]If you have more than one skimmer, obviously, clean them all.
- ✓ If your skimmer baskets are extremely full or hard

---

[53]   Kafko/Equator   Skimmer   Basket,   find   replacements   at AskthePoolGuy.com

to remove, turn OFF your pump to release the suction.

✓ During the fall check your skimmer baskets often. You may think, we are not swimming, I don't have to worry about the pool, however your pump which may strain with improper water flow may prematurely age or become damaged if left unchecked.

Notes for Above Ground Pools:
To access your skimmer you may need to remove the basket from the skimmer opening itself, or from the lid mounted outside the pool wall. While servicing your above ground pool you may want to have plugs handy to plug the skimmer outlet at the bottom of the skimmer, or the pool return lines, depending on how your pool was built.

54

Brushing your Pool

Pool brushes are usually long and have durable nylon bristles which can be used on any type of pool. Stainless steel bristled brushes are only for gunite pools (also referred to as concrete, shotcrete or pebble surfaced pools).

Brushing is important for your pool. At first glance if your pool appears clean, you may decide to skip this step, however, if you

---

54 Above Ground Swimming Pool with Wooden Deck Surround

don't have an automatic pool cleaner scrubbing your pool floor and walls, algae can start to form and cause the surface to be slippery, even before you notice any change.

Brushing removes microscopic debris and matter from the pool walls and floor and will suspend it into the water where it can either be circulated through the filter and removed from the pool, or killed by your sanitizing system and the remains filtered out.

If you brush the pool you may notice the pool get cloudy if you have microscopic matter that is released from the pool surface. You can use a clarifier or flocculant that will coagulate smaller particles together to be filtered out of the pool, or clumped together and settle to the bottom to be vacuumed out.

NOTE: If the microscopic matter is too small and remains in the pool, you will need to add a Clarifier to coagulate these small particles into larger particles, where they will indeed be killed by chlorine (or its alternative) and trapped by the filter.

Brush the pool walls first, and the floor second, pushing debris toward the main drain, starting at the shallow end.

When possible, brush one day and allow the debris to settle and vacuum the following day. Run the pump and filter after brushing the pool to allow the filtration system to remove as much debris as possible. In cases where you need to floc the pool and you need debris to settle you may need to turn the pool system off. Refer to product directions for proper use.

An alternative to brushing is to get a Dolphin pool cleaner that will scrub the pool walls and floor for you, removing much of the need for your manual brushing.

You can also hire a pool company to perform a weekly cleaning and maintenance visit for your pool.

Vacuuming

Some of this process is covered in the "Brushing" section because vacuuming usually comes after brushing, just like in this book and the dictionary.

Vacuuming "On Filter"

During your regular vacuuming, you will want your multi-port in the filter position. This will vacuum the debris from the bottom of the pool and push the water through the filter for removal. If you are vacuuming and you notice debris flowing back into the pool you will want to clean the filter, and backwash a sand or DE filter. If you have continued issue with fine debris returning to the pool consider using a clarifier or flocculant, or vacuuming the pool to waste and bypassing the filter. This will remove water from your pool so be prepared to refill the pool, or even add water before you vacuum so you have room to remove some of the water.

Types of Vac Heads

[55]Use the right type of vac head for your pool. Vinyl liner vac heads are typically triangle or oval shaped, with brushes on the bottom.

Gunite vac heads are flat with rollers and no brushes on the bottom.

---

[55] Triangle Vinyl Vac Head with Bottom Brushes

56

If you have a hybrid swimming pool and want to manually vacuum, be sure to only use a vinyl vac head on the vinyl portion of your pool and the vinyl or a gunite head on the gunite portion of your pool.

Steps for Vacuuming:

- ✓ Brush the pool down the day before you vacuum when possible. Allow the filter to operate to remove brushed particulate from the pool.
- ✓ In cases of cloudy water consider adding a clarifier or a flocculant to the pool (but not both at the same time unless the instructions on the bottle direct you to).
- ✓ Allow the pool water to settle by turning the pool off overnight.
- ✓ When you go to vacuum, make sure the water level in your pool is high enough to allow you to vacuum and backwash. Add water prior to vacuuming if you think you will need the additional water level.
- ✓ Determine which valve at your equipment pad is your main drain, and which is your skimmer. (Quick tip: when Ask the Pool Girl opened and closed pools she added a zip tie to the pipe to

---

56 Gunite Vac Head with Rollers

indicate the skimmer. This wasn't easily removed from the pool so at a glance and without guessing it was easy to determine the skimmer line. It also lasted longer than sharpie marker or stickers.)

✓ Remove the skimmer basket from the skimmer where you will set up the vacuum.

✓ Close the valve for the main drain to increase suction through the skimmer line that you will be using to vacuum.

✓ [57]Grab your Vac Pole
✓ Install a vacpole to your vac head.
✓ Install the end of the vacuum hose that swivels to the vac head that will go into the pool.
✓ Allow the vac head and hose to sink to the bottom of the pool.
✓ Continuing with the vac hose, push it a foot at a time into the water, beginning with the end in the pool and concluding with the other end of the hose. Refer to our online tutorials @askthepoolguy on YouTube for demonstrations on how this is done to correctly prime the hose and fill it with water.
✓ Don't as one customer asked use your household vacuum to vacuum your pool!
✓ The goal is to have no air in the vacuum hose when you go to attach it to the hole in the bottom of the skimmer, or to the vac plate.
✓ Be careful not to fall into the pool or you look silly, and be wet.

---

[57] Telescoping VacPole

✓ [58]Once the vac hose is completely filled with water, quickly install the end of the vac hose into the skimmer hole or onto the vac plate on top of your skimmer basket.

✓ Using the vac pole, begin to vacuum by slowly pushing the vac head across the pool floor. Make sure the suction is not too strong that the vac head is getting stuck, or sucking up any vinyl liner.

[59] If your suction is too strong, re-open up the main drain valve a little.

✓ As you vacuum, the dirt you vacuum up will get trapped in the filter. This may cause the pressure in the filter to rise. As you notice the suction decrease, or the pressure on your pressure gauge going up to 10 psi above your  normal operating pressure, then clean the filter. If your pool is very dirty, you may need to repeat the backwashing process several times during your vacuuming.

✓ Vacuum slowly, with the vac head flush on the floor of the pool.

✓ Do not lift the vac head out of the water, as it will introduce air into the pump and cause a loss of suction.

---

[58] Equator/Kafko Vac Plate for use with an Equator/Kafko Skimmer Basket
[59] Vacuum Hose for use in any type of swimming pool

✓ Sometimes people will hold the end of the vac hose in front of a return jet to prime the hose (eliminate the air and fill with water). This is an option, just be careful that you don't stir up the water on the pool floor too much with the water pushing back through the hose. Cleaning is the objective not making the pool harder to clean.

Vacuum "To Waste"

Sometimes you will not want to put the vacuum debris through your filter, in cases of thick and heavy sediment or algae. If this is the case, you can turn your multi-port to waste and allow the water to leave the pool and bypass the filter. This will also drain your pool, so make sure you start with enough water, and add more as your water level begins to decrease.

NOTE: Your pool pump and vacuum will waste water from your pool quickly, much more quickly than your garden hose can add it, so be prepared to monitor your hose for quite some time if you need to add water. In the case of automatic water Levolor®[60], they may only run for a set amount of time each day, if your need for water exceeds what the program will add you may need to add some with the hose and monitor it yourself.

IMPORTANT: NEVER, ever, allow your water level to drop below the skimmer while your pump is running. This will allow air into your system which will often cause a loss of prime or worse, it could cause your motor to overheat or become defective and need to be replaced.

There are new pumps on the market that are now air cooled, instead of the industry standard water cooled pumps, so the good news is those pumps will be less affected by the loss of prime, however your pool filter will still be affected.

---

[60] Levolor® K-1100 www.**jandy**.com/en/products/water-leveling/k1100

Vacuuming An Aboveground Pool

Vacuuming an above ground pool is similar to vacuuming an inground pool. Above ground pools are usually vinyl lined, so use the vinyl liner vac head.

Be very careful that you don't vacuum an above ground pool to waste and lose too much water. Above ground pools are especially sensitive structurally to having the right amount of water in them at all times.

Advantages of Automatic Pool Cleaners

Some people can find their Zen while vacuuming a swimming pool. If you are not one of those people, read on, we have some options for you.

Automatic pool cleaners are a great solution for keeping the pool vacuumed, as well as the walls brushed, and the water moving.

[61]There are several different types of pool cleaners, and we do have a clear favorite.

Pressure Side Cleaner

These automatic cleaners attach to the return side of your pool's circulation system. These cleaners are powered by the water being pushed back into the pool because they have their own hydraulic power system encased inside. Because these units are on the pressure side of the circulation system they have advantages. They help to distribute clean water throughout the pool, and because they have their own debris bag they do not  interfere with the filter system. Even if the debris bag gets full the cleaner will still operate, it just won't pick up any more debris.

Suction Side Automatic Pool Cleaner

Unlike the pressure side automatic pool cleaner, suction side cleaners attach to the suction side of your plumbing. This means it attaches to the pipes and fittings which bring water

---

[61] Polaris Automatic Pool Cleaner - Pressure Side Cleaner

from the pool to the pump and equipment. They typically attach to one of the suction ports at the pool (like the skimmer or vacuum port) so the cleaner's hose can attach. When the hose is attached and the filter pump is [62]running suction is created on the bottom of the cleaner. This causes the cleaner to move automatically and

randomly around the pool floor with motions created by a device in the cleaner. Debris is then sucked up through the neck into the hose and stops at the filter pump strainer basket.

[63]Robotic Pool Cleaner

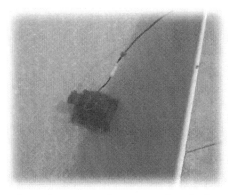

Robotic cleaners are actually electric cleaners with a transformer plugged into a regular wall outlet. Electricity and water usually don't go well together; this is an exception because of the power transformer box. They are perfectly safe when used properly. It has a pump motor that draws debris into the unit's filter and a drive motor which makes it able to move around the pool. These cleaners have a separate filter and can be cleaned with ease. Some robotic cleaners even come with remotes and can be controlled from your lounge chair, it doesn't get better than that. These are usually the most costly of automatic cleaners.

Choosing an Automatic Pool Cleaner

All three of these cleaners will work well for your pool. Suction side cleaners may need backwashing, while pressure side

---

[62] Above Ground automatic Pool Cleaner
[63] Dolphin Robotic Pool Cleaner

cleaners work off the return line of your pool. Suction side automatic cleaners might be the cheapest while the robotic cleaners will be more expensive.

[64]You could always hire a pool professional or neighbor kid to clean your pool for you on a regular basis. Whichever option you choose, you'll need to choose some way of regularly keeping your pool vacuumed, brushed, and cleaned.

Dolphin Pool Cleaner

[65]The pool guy's favorite automatic pool cleaner has always been the Dolphin™ by Maytronics[ix].

They do have an up-front cost, so even if it means waiting a year and saving up your money to invest in one, consider this.

When purchasing a Dolphin, we do recommend buying these from a pool professional because the online options either don't come with the right warranties, or you may get something that could damage the surface of your pool. We have seen people get the wrong type or something the internet

---

[64] Manual Pool Cleaning by Mark, Service Team Leader, Ask the Pool Guy
[65] Dolphin Robotic Pool Cleaner

claimed would work that caused issues on their pool liner or pool surface.

The average life span for a pool cleaner is 5-6 years, however if you have bad water chemistry you will shorten this, or with correct use and care, they may last longer.

[66]It is a self contained unit that has a power center – you can also get one that is cordless and remote controlled – so the debris goes right into the bag in the unit itself. We believe it is by far the best cleaner on the market because it doesn't interfere with your filtration system, you don't need additional ports or returns in your pool for it to work, it will filter the water internally and trap debris for easy use and cleaning, and it will climb walls and scrub the pool surface and tile line, all reducing the amount of brushing and vacuuming you will need to   do   by hand.

[66] The Pool Guy, a Self Portrait

Monthly Maintenance

Deck Equipment - Pool Handrails & Ladders

[67]Typically deck equipment refers to handrails and ladders. They are often made of stainless steel. If your pool is a salt pool you may notice corrosion of your handrail or ladder stainless steel, or of your  deck anchors if your pool equipment isn't done properly with a zinc anode to prevent electrolysis. Watch for this, especially in a salt water pool. You can clean your deck equipment with a metal cleaner (just prevent this from getting into the pool.) Some kitchen cleaners (such as Mr. Clean Magic Erasers) will be okay to use on your deck equipment. See the section on Zinc anodes if you see signs of oxidation or pitting.

Pool Tile or Liner

[68]The tile line on a gunite or hybrid swimming pool acts as an area to hide the "bathtub line" that forms from fluctuations in the water level of your pool, and of deposits of minerals and grime on the surface.

Clean your tile by brushing regularly.

---

[67] Handrails on a Gunite Pool
[68] Cleaning the tile and marcite on a gunite pool with muriatic acid during an acid wash

In a gunite/tile pool you can pour chlorine directly on the tile and scrub, and in extreme cases you can use muriatic acid as well. You can also use tools made specifically for tile cleaning. Tile cleaning should be done regularly, as you notice that it needs it. You may notice insoluble suntan lotions and body oils add to the need for cleaning, which is one of the reasons showering before entering a pool is important. You can find products specific to tile line cleaning from your pool supplier.

[69]

---

[69] The waterline on Ceramic Tile

Monthly Sample Testing
of your Pool Water Chemistry

Pool Water Chemistry is really the most important preventative maintenance you can perform for your pool, as well as monitoring your water level and pool equipment operation.

Again, find a good pool store in your area where you can bring in a water sample once a month for a computerized test of your chemicals and recommendations beyond your regular at home water testing.

70

---

[70] Checking water chemistry during a weekly service visit

More Maintenance Tips

In addition to routine maintenance, these are maintenance items that will help your equipment run properly.

Lubricating O-Rings

[71]A water based lubricant for your equipment plugs and o-rings will be a great product to use during pool openings, and while performing maintenance to your pump lid and o-ring. As you clean your pump basket and replace the lid to prime your pump, lubricate the o-ring if you have any air leaks or trouble with priming. This will help the lid to seal properly and eliminate air or water leaks. Do NOT use petroleum jelly, it is not a good product for your swimming pool equipment.

Regular Use Of The Heater

You will prolong the life of your heater by using it. If the heater is left unused, spiders and other insects, as well as rodents, dirt, and rust may take up residence in your heater. The best maintenance for your heater is to use it. If you do attempt to use your heater and have issues with it running or firing, always check your filter function first, and perform a filter cleaning or backwash.

[72]Heaters have an internal pressure switch that only allows the heater to turn on when the water pressure registers correctly. If your flow is low due to a dirty or

---

[71] Magic Lube - Silicone Based Lubricant formulated for swimming pool equipment
[72] Service Team Leader Mark servicing a Raypak Pool Heater

clogged filter, your heater will not fire.

If you have any other issues with your heater, we suggest calling a pool professional for service and help with your heater issue diagnosis.

Pool Deck Maintenance

It is a good idea to rinse down or sweep your pool deck, especially if you notice rocks, gravel, dirt, grass clippings or other debris. You want to keep this in your yard, and out of your pool. If you leave debris on your pool deck and it rains, you want to prevent any runoff from getting into your pool.

Debris that blows into your pool may:

- ✓ cause more need for chemicals to mitigate the debris in the pool
- ✓ fall to the pool floor and cause the need for additional vacuuming
- ✓ fill up your skimmer and/or pump baskets

Winter Maintenance in Southern Climates

During the winter months in southern climates, keep your chemicals balanced and your pool clean. This will prevent stains in your pool, as well as prevent scaling, etching and other pool damage.

In freezing temperatures when the pool equipment is circulating and the pool is clean there should be enough water movement to prevent freezing issues. If you are concerned about freezing, turn your heater to a temperature that will prevent freezing temperatures from affecting your pool water. Most new pool pumps have freeze prevention built in and should kick on to circulate the water if they measure a temperature drop. Of course, if your power goes out, then even this won't help.

To operate your pool during the winter:

- ✓ Maintain your pool water chemistry and check your water on a regular basis.
- ✓ Keep your skimmer and pump baskets free of debris.
- ✓ Regularly backwash your sand or DE filter
- ✓ Drain any pumps that are not continually circulating such as an unused pool sweep.
- ✓ In case of an electrical outage, drain the filter and pump by removing the drain plugs, this will allow water to drain out to prevent it from freezing and damaging your equipment.

Frosty, Photo credit, Scott Gafford

Maintaining Great Water Chemistry

We get a lot of Ask the Pool Guy questions about what the proper water chemistry levels are for a swimming pool.

Many pool builders offer a new owner training lesson, and it is important to take advantage of this. If you purchase a home with an existing pool, check around for a pool company in your area that will offer a new pool owner lesson, often for the price of a service call, or with Ask the Pool Guy, complimentary as part of a pool opening service.

[73]Maintaining the correct water chemistry is unique to each pool, within a certain set of guidelines. Since the equipment used on each pool is specific to the pool, it is important to learn what your pool will require.

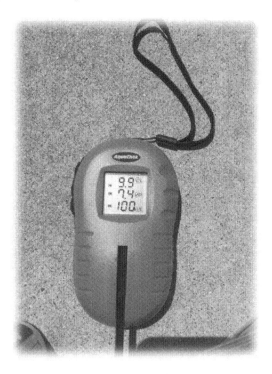

---

[73] AquaChek's TruTest, a pool side water testing system for accurate readings

Test Kit Essentials

Choose a test kit that is simple to use, and easy to interpret. We suggest the AquaChek 5 or 7 in 1 test strips, or the TruTest (pictured) to help make taking your readings simple.

The most important things to note about your swimming pool water chemistry:

- ✓ Follow manufacturer directions for testing your water.
- ✓ When you need to add chemicals, read the label about the proper way to add the chemicals to your pool.
- ✓ When you need to add chemicals, cut the doses in half, and add half at a time, allow time to circulate and recheck.
- ✓ Keep a record, especially when you are learning, or having trouble keeping your water clear. This will help for troubleshooting.
- ✓ ALWAYS know what chemicals to add in the proper order. DO NOT just dump two different chemicals in the pool at the same time, they could react together and cause issues you don't want to have.

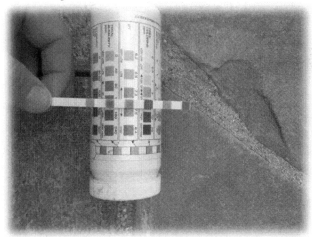

74

---

[74] AquaChek test strip reading high chlorine

Swimming Pool Water Chemistry Numbers

Ask the Pool Guy's Ideal Numbers for Water Chemistry

- ✓ FCL 1.0-3.0 ppm (free chlorine)
- ✓ pH 7.4-7.6
- ✓ TA or ALK 80-120 (Total Alkalinity)
- ✓ CH 200-350 Gunite Pools or 150-200 Vinyl Pools, 200-250 for Hybrid Swimming Pools (Calcium Hardness)
- ✓ CYA 30-60 (Cyanuric Acid/Stabilizer)
- ✓ TDS <1500 in non salt pools, the lower the number the better (Total Dissolved Solids)
- ✓ Salt - per manufacturer directions for your chlorine generator

Reading your test strip

Dip and swirl per manufacturer directions. Read the strip immediately to match the colors to determine your levels.

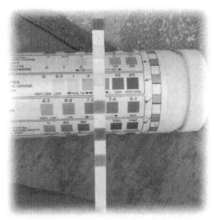

75

To remedy this situation you would need to add chlorine, and watch the pH in a few days to keep it in the optimal range.

---

[75] AquaChek test strip reading no chlorine and high pH/Alkalinity

Fresh Clear Pretty Water Still Needs to Be Balanced!

If you start with fresh water, just because the water looks clear doesn't mean it is balanced. If you have an acid wash performed, a vinyl liner replacement, or have refilled your pool for any reason you MUST BALANCE your water. We have had homeowners who have done the above renovations, and thought clear water meant healthy water - months later when their vinyl liner was completely bleached, or their stainless steel screws were rusting out completely realized they should not have ignored their water chemistry!

76

We recommend testing your water once per week with test strips for a test kit, and bring a water sample to your local pool store once per month during the summer for comprehensive computerized water testing.

Swimming pools with water chemistry issues will result in wrinkled liners, rusting stainless steel screws in the skimmer,

---

[76] Stainless Steel Corrosion from extremely aggressive water due to low alkalinity and pH (6 month exposure)

return fittings, and lights, and etching or staining and deposits in the surface of gunite/pebble/marcite pools, as well as deterioration of your metals in your pool equipment, all of which can be costly to fix, and can be prevented!

Water Chemistry Quick Reference Targets:

- ➢ FCL 1.0-3.0 ppm
- ➢ pH 7.4-7.6 (7.4 is the ideal number for swimmer comfort, as it is the same pH in the human eyes and mucous membranes)
- ➢ TA or ALK 80-120 (Salt water Pools, Keep Alkalinity at 80-100 to keep your pH from bouncing)
- ➢ CH 200-350 Gunite Pools or 150-200
- ➢ CH Vinyl Pools, 200-250 Hybrid Pools
- ➢ CYA 30-60
- ➢ TDS <1500 in non salt pools, the lower the number the better
- ➢ Salt - Per Manufacturer Recommendations

77

---

[77] Green means go on this clever system to let neighbors know when the pool is open.

Chlorine Quick Tips

What is the Best Type of Chlorine for My Pool?

Well, if you have a salt swimming pool, a saltwater pool, you're actually generating chlorine.

Chlorine is the best, most readily-available sanitizing method for swimming pools. If you don't have a salt generator on your pool, then what you should have is some type of automatic chlorine dispenser.

CL220 - Automatic Chlorinator

The CL220 made by Hayward is the tank that you put chlorine tablets in, and it's plumbed into your system, so it dissolves them out and disperses them into your water when your system is running.

[78]If you have the automatic chlorinator, the CL220, you'll want to monitor that and test your water regularly to make sure that you maintain a residual of 1-3 parts per million of chlorine in your water, so that it can do its efficient sanitizing. We also recommend that you shock the pool once a week. Shocking the pool  would consist of adding either pouches of shock, but be careful that you get the right kind for your pool, because if you just throw granular shock into a vinyl liner swimming pool and it's Cal-Hypo, for example, it's slower dissolving. If that lands on the bottom of the pool, you could have some potential bleaching or staining occur from the addition of that chlorine.

---

[78] Hayward CL220 Inline Chlorinator - Chlorine Tablet Dispenser

If you're going to shock a vinyl liner pool, you'll want a non-chlorine based shock and oxidizer, or you'll want to dissolve your chlorine in a bucket before you add it to the pool.

Floater

Another way that you can add chlorine to your pool is to have a floater. The floater is one of those plastic containers that you fill up with chlorine tablets, toss it in the pool, and it disperses the chlorine as it floats around the pool.

79

If you do use a floater in your pool, you'll want to make sure that you monitor the output on those. Typically, you can spin the bottom and open it or close it just a little bit.

You'll want to make sure that you have a nice amount of chlorine always in the floater, and if you notice that your water is getting too much, like if it's dissolving too quickly, then you'll want to tighten or spin that so that it's letting a little bit less of the chlorine through. Of course, with a floater you have it in the

---

79 Floating Chlorine Tablet Dispenser in a Vinyl Liner Pool

water, and sometimes kids like to play with those, we don't advise that as they are dispersing chlorine and the amount can be quite concentrated in the feeder.

Chlorine Generator

The chlorine generator of the saltwater system is going to give you the softest water. It's going to be a more saline solution, so it's really comfortable for swimmers to swim in. The other benefit of that is you don't have to be adding additional chlorine to your pool, simply by adding the salt and allowing the generator to do its work, it'll be sanitizing the pool water for you.

Most chlorine generating systems have different settings, so you can set the chlorine generator to work at a certain percentage. We tend to use the Pentair IntelliChlor system, and depending on what's needed for each individual pool the settings will vary a little bit. There are different size cells for different size pools. An IC20 will chlorinate 20,000 gallons of water running 24 hours a day. The IC40 will chlorinate 40,000 gallons of water running 24 hours a day.

[80]The chlorine generators are only making chlorine when the swimming pool is running. If you have a swimming pool that's kind of in the middle of those sizes, always go a size up. If you're under 20,000 gallons, the IC20 would work, if you're over 20,000, under 40k, that would work. In a case where you have a much larger pool than that, you might actually need to install two

---

[80] IntelliChlor Salt Generator - all systems go at 60% production

chlorine generating units to take care of the chlorine demand that you'll have for your pool.

Liquid Chlorine

The quickest and easiest way to shock a pool is by using liquid chlorine. Here's a fun fact that I hadn't known until recently about liquid chlorine. It's not available in some locations. Some states actually have transportation laws that make it difficult to transport liquid chlorine. If you're in a state where liquid chlorine is readily available, quickest and easiest way to shock your pool, however, not the best for long-term sanitizing, as the liquid chlorine doesn't last long in the pool, and is used up quickly by the sun and organic material. A slow release form of chlorine is best for long term sanitizing.

81

Shock Cloudy Pool Water

Liquid chlorine works really quickly at cleaning up your pool. If my pool ever starts to look a little bit cloudy, or the water gets a little bit dull, what I'll typically do is backwash my pool, because I have a sand filter, backwash the pool water, and then add liquid chlorine. In my pool, typically one or two gallons does the trick, overnight, it'll clear things up.

---

81 Pool Shock - Liquid Chlorine a super fast acting chlorine source

Liquid chlorine is fast-acting. It's also fast to be used up. When it is sanitizing your pool water, it's getting used, or if sunlight hits it, it's very unstable and it won't stay and remain in the water. If it's a hot summer day and the sun is beating down on it, you're actually using up quite a bit of that chlorine. If you're going to use chlorine, it's a fast-acting method to get a very quick fix, but then you also need to address your long-term sanitizing issues.

Water Chemistry Definitions:

Brief History of Chlorine

Chlorine was discovered in 1774 by a chemist from Sweden named Carl Scheele. He mixed the element Chlorine with a powdered pryslusite into muriatic acid.

Chlorine was then named 'chlorine' because of its greenish color- stemming from the Greek word for green, "Khloros".

How is Chlorine Made?

Today chlorine is produced by the electrolysis of salt water.

"Chlorine is formed when electricity is passed through 2NaCl (salt) and 2H2o (water), the atoms dissociate into C12 (chlorine) + 2NaOH (sodium hydroxide) + H2 (hydrogen). In the manufacture of chlorine, C12 is isolated in its gaseous form, and used to create other chlorine compounds used for sanitizing, bleaching, and production of plastics and related products."[x] (www.poolcenter.com)

Chlorine as a Sanitizer

When chlorine is added to water, a chemical reaction occurs. This reaction leaves us with hypochlorous acid and hydrochloric acid (HOCl & HCl). Hypochlorous acid is the active chlorine. It is what does the hard sanitizing work in your pool. Different amounts of each chemical are created, and it depends on your water temperature and your water pH levels. The chlorine molecules kill microorganisms my 'slashing' through the cell. It destroys the inner enzymes. When this occurs, the cell is basically deactivated. The hypochlorous molecule continues slashing through all these cells until it combines with a nitrogen or ammonia compound. Sometimes it becomes a chloramine, and sometimes it is broken down (deactivating itself).

How Dangerous is Chlorine?

Like all chemical compounds, chlorine has the ability to be potentially very hazardous. Some forms of it are more dangerous than others. However, the chlorine found in water in swimming pools poses no danger for swimmers at all.

Some people may find they have an allergic reaction to chlorine, however these are rare. If you have a poorly balanced pool, chloramines may form. This can cause red eyes in swimmers but it is not dangerous. If you have a pool with extremely high levels of chlorine, it is possible the water could release enough gas from the surface to cause breathing difficulties- especially in an indoor pool. This is also unlikely.

The main hazard chlorine poses is to the one who handles it regularly and administers it to the pool.

If that is you, use caution and always read the directions on the label. When you open a container of chlorine, use caution. Breathing in straight chlorine can make you unconscious. It could even be fatal. We recommend ALWAYS wearing gloves and eye protection of some sort when handling chlorine. If it touches your skin accidentally, you should wash it off to prevent irritations. If you get chlorine splashed in your eye, wash your eye with water and contact a doctor right away. The most important thing to remember when handling chlorine is to **NEVER MIX IT WITH ANY OTHER CHEMICAL**. Mixing chlorine with any other chemical could produce very bad reactions. This can cause serious health problems, and any explosions can be extremely dangerous. To protect yourself and your family, store chlorine away from other chemicals and keep out of the reach of children.

All About Chlorine[xi]

Have you ever gone to a hotel or natatorium and been almost knocked off your feet by the chlorine smell in the air? Many people believe that the smell of chlorine in the air means that the pool is "clean" or even "healthy." Well, that's not entirely true. That chlorine smell is "used chlorine", meaning chlorine that has already done its job of sanitizing, used chlorine is known as *combined chlorine* or *chloramine*. Chloramines, in high doses, can actually be toxic to swimmers.

Shocking or ***oxidizing*** (synonymous) the pool is needed when there is a combined chlorine reading in the water. To understand this process, there are a couple things about chlorine that you should know:

In testing your pool there are three chlorine based readings you need to know.

Free Available Chlorine (FAC) is the measurement of chlorine in the water that has not been used yet, it's "free" to do its job sanitizing or oxidizing.

Total Chlorine (TC) is the measurement of all the sanitizer or oxidizer in the water.

Combined Chlorine (CC) is the difference between the two. It signifies the chlorine that has already been used. This is the chloramine reading.

TC – FAC = CC

If there is a difference between the FAC and the TC that is greater than .3 parts per million (ppm) than you need to oxidize the pool water. In oxidization, the combined chlorine that is in the water is oxidized so that it can off gas and leave only free chlorine (chlorine that has not been used) in the pool.

In order to achieve this oxidization, you must use enough chlorine to reach *Breakpoint Chlorination.* This is achieved when you put in enough chlorine to reach ten times (10x) the amount of your combined chlorine reading.

There are many ways to oxidize your pool water to reach Breakpoint Chlorination. Let's discuss the two main ways; chlorine shock and non-chlorine shock.

Chlorine Shock:

There are many types of chlorine shock; liquid chlorine (sodium hypochlorite), cal-hypo (calcium hypochlorite), and lithium (lithium hypochlorite). Each one of these shocks will do the trick but there are inherent differences between them all.

Liquid chlorine is relatively inexpensive, has a high pH (>13), which can be detrimental in high doses, turns to salt water once finished oxidizing, and an available chlorine of 10-12% (laundry bleach has approximately 4%), but has a low dosage rate to achieve Breakpoint at 1 gallon of liquid chlorine per 10k gallons of pool water. No swimming for approximately 24 hours.

Cal-Hypo is relatively inexpensive, has a high pH (<11), an available chlorine of 65-75%, can increase your calcium hardness level with prolonged use, but has a low dosage rate of to achieve Breakpoint at anywhere from 1# per 10k-15k gallons depending on the available chlorine percentage. No swimming for approximately 24 hours.

Lithium is the most expensive of the chlorine shocks, dissolves on contact, has a high pH (<10.5), an available chlorine of 29%, leaves no residue, but has a high dosage rate to achieve Breakpoint at 1# per 8k gallons. No swimming for approximately 24 hours.

To achieve Breakpoint Chlorination, homeowners must know their pools total gallons because if you treat a 22k gallon pool with enough shock to reach Breakpoint for a 20k pool, you are not going to reach Breakpoint but actually make matters worse by increasing the combined chlorine reading. That is where Non-Chlorine Shock comes in.

Non-Chlorine Shock:

Non-Chlorine Shock, also known as Oxone™, Potassium Monopersulfate or Potassium Peroxymonosulfate, abbreviated MPS, is totally soluble (dissolves on contact), leaves no residue, has a pH of 9, is relatively inexpensive, has a dosage rate of 1# per 10k gallons of pool water, swimming can resume in 15 minutes, and, most importantly, will oxidize chloramines without needing to reach Breakpoint chlorination. Multiple doses may be necessary if the Combined Chlorine reading is above 2ppm.

In conclusion, there are a couple things to note. If your pool has algae, use a chlorine based shock, MPS will not kill algae.

If your pool starts to get hazy, you can use either, but be sure to use any chlorinated shock once the sun is not shining on the pool. UV rays from the sun will shorten the life of chlorinated shocks.

Non-Chlorine shock can be used at any time so long as swimmers wait at least 15 minutes before swimming. Non-chlorine shock will not bleach out liners, swim trunks, etc. where if you use chlorinated shocks you should wait until the chlorine level has dropped to normal levels of 2-4ppm of FAC/TC, which is approximately 18-24 hours later depending on the amount of contaminants you are trying to oxidize and the time of day the chlorinated shocks are added to the pool.

FC – Free Chlorine – Free chlorine kills bacteria and oxidizes contaminants in the water. Chlorine must continually be replenished, once it kills bacteria it is used up.

Keeping the free chlorine level is the most important part of keeping your water balanced and for the prevention of algae.

Free chlorine should be tested and added daily. An automatic chlorinator (when functioning properly) will release a consistent amount of chlorine into your pool. Salt water generators will also release a consistent amount of chlorine in your pool water. Remember, both of these systems will only release chlorine if your pool is running, so make sure it runs the required amount of hours in a day to keep up with your chlorine demand.

The level of free chlorine available in your pool will be influenced by the amount of CYA in your pool, and both should be kept at idea levels.

Forms of Chlorine

Chlorine comes in many forms including 3 or 1-inch tablets, liquid, sticks, bottles, or in granules. You can also produce chlorine in your pool through the use of a chlorine generator/salt system.

Liquid Chlorine

Liquid Chlorine is the best choice for fast acting results.

It is less stable than tablets which often have stabilizer added to reduce the sun's effect on the chlorine.

If you have a pool turning cloudy and green, and liquid chlorine is available in your state (some states transportation laws prevent liquid chlorine from being available), shocking your pool with a gallon or two will usually do the trick. For steady doses and continual sanitizing of your pool, keep reading.

Tablets 3" and 1" and Sticks

The most common and least expensive form of chlorine are the 3-inch tablets because they are slow to dissolve and require little maintenance. Chlorine sticks dissolve even slower than the 3-inch tablets but are not as common. A concentration of about 90% Trichloro-S-Triazinetrione is ideal. These two types of chlorine are best suited for in-ground pools.

Granular chlorine works just as well as the above mentioned, but you must always dissolve inorganic chlorine such as granules, in a bucket of water first before adding to the pool. Granular chlorine should have a 56% – 62% concentration of Sodium Dichloro-S-Triazinetrione. This type of chlorine must be added to the pool almost daily and have daily testing.

1-inch tablets are best suited for above ground pools, smaller in-ground pools, and spas.

TIP: Be sure to purchase your tablets or sticks from a pool supply store. You may find chlorine tablets and sticks cheaper at a "big box" chain, but the quality goes way down. There will be filler agents and they will dissolve and crumble much faster.

Chlorinators or Chlorine Feeders

Once you have the correct chlorine for your pool, you will need to add it to the pool water. Automatic chlorine feeders or floating feeders make for much less maintenance. They slowly dissolve the chlorine tablets or sticks and disperse the proper amount of chlorine needed for your pool. If the feeder is adjusted correctly, you should be able to go a week or more before checking your feeder.

Tablets in Skimmers? = NO

Sometimes pool owners try a shortcut and add tablets to their pool skimmer. *Please DON'T!* This will add high concentrations of chlorine into your pool plumbing and force high levels through your heater. This can contribute to major damage and corrosion to **your heater internals, and is a very costly issue to have.**

Granular Chlorine and Vinyl Liner Pools

If using granular products, they must be pre-dissolved in a bucket of water first. NOTE: Be sure to fill the bucket with water first, before adding the granules to avoid splashing or harm. You can then pour the bucket around the perimeter of the pool focusing the majority towards the deep end.

Brush the pool after adding so the granules don't have chance to settle and burn or bleach the pool surface especially in vinyl liner pools.

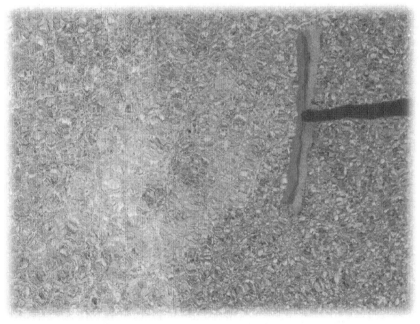

82

---

[82] Chlorine granular shock permanently bleached this vinyl liner

TC – Total Chlorine – When your free chlorine combines with contaminants it becomes combined chlorine, or chloramines. Combined chlorine has almost no ability to sanitize or oxidize your water (basically, it can't do its job in this form).

This form of chlorine has little to no ability to sanitize or oxidize your water. Total Chlorine is the sum of combined chlorine and free chlorine. If you get the traditional chlorine smell, especially in indoor (hotel) pools, it means you don't have enough chlorine in the pool that can do its job, and too much total chlorine. To fix this issue, the pool should be shocked to break point chlorination to break the bonds and allow free chlorine to get back to doing its job.

Superchlorination or "Shocking"

Perspiration and urine in a pool causes ammonia (a source of nitrogen). This nitrogen will react to the chorine to form chloramines (combined chlorine). When the chloramines are high, the swimmer will have irritation to the eyes and the chlorine will smell very strong. You may think that there is too much chlorine in the pool, when actually the opposite is true. The pool needs to be "shocked" by raising the chlorine residual by 5 to 10 times the normal level. Depending on the level of activity in your pool, "shocking" will need to be done once a week to once every couple of weeks preferably at night.

TA – Total Alkalinity – Alkalinity is the total measure of alkaline substances in water, and the ability of water to neutralize acid or resist or buffer pH changes.

> Total Alkalinity level help the water buffer pH changes.
> Buffering means it will take a larger quantity of a chemical to change the pH.
> When Total Alkalinity levels are low, pH levels will fluctuate wildly.
> At high Total Alkalinity levels, pH will tend to rise gradually, or drift up.

Total Alkalinity is increased by adding sodium bicarbonate (baking soda/soda ash) and decreased by adding sodium bisulfate or muriatic acid.

Please note you *Always adjust TA before adjusting pH.*

Total Alkalinity, or TA, should usually be kept at 80 – 120 ppm, and right between 80-100ppm as the ideal in salt water swimming pools.

Low Total Alkalinity

Low total alkalinity may cause:

> [83]etching of the plaster, pebble, marcite or tile/grout
> corrosion of metal parts, especially copper in the heater core, stainless steel screws or light rings, and other metal parts on either your pool or equipment
> staining of the pool's

---

[83] Corrosion of the pool light and staining on the vinyl liner from aggressive water with low alkalinity and low pH (exposure 6 months)

surfaces by corroding metal and depositing it on pool surfaces

➢ green water - there is a difference between the dull metallic green color of low alkalinity and pH and the fluorescent green of iron in the water, or the deep green of an algae issue. As you become familiar with your pool you will be able to spot these subtle color changes.

➢ burning eyes and itchy skin

➢ pH bounce (rapid fluctuations in pH)

Raising low total alkalinity

Sodium bicarbonate (bicarb) will raise the total alkalinity of your pool water, without raising the pH (much).

pH plus will raise the pH as well as the alkalinity

Increase your total alkalinity over a period of time (one or more days) adding one pound of bicarb for 6,000 gallons of water.

High Total Alkalinity

High Alkalinity may cause:

➢ pH remaining at high levels even when you try to reduce it with pH minus

➢ cloudy water

➢ burning eyes and itchy skin

➢ chlorine to be less efficient and encouraging algae growth

➢ [84]in combination with high pH, high alkalinity can contribute to a slippery or slimy pool surface, and

---

[84] Cloudy pool water - swimming is not advisable when you cannot see the bottom of the pool. Scale may start forming at this point as well.

scaling and deposits on pool surfaces

Alkalinity does not have to be tested for as often as pH. It is a measure of the buffering capacity or the ability of pool water to resist a change in pH, therefore good Total Alkalinity will make it much easier to maintain good pH.

The appropriate range for Total Alkalinity in pool water is between 75 and 120 ppm (parts per million). High Total Alkalinity (above 120 ppm) will allow your pH to slowly creep up and resist efforts to change.

Low Total Alkalinity (below 75 ppm) allows your pH to "bounce" from one extreme to the other, making it very difficult to keep your pH in the appropriate range.

> ➢ Total Alkalinity, or TA, should usually be kept at 80 – 120 ppm, and right between 80-100ppm as the ideal in salt water swimming pools.

Lowering high total alkalinity

Adding small amounts of a pH minus product will introduce acid to reduce the pH while also lowering the total alkalinity, muriatic acid can also be used. Some pool equipment pads are equipped with an acid dispenser which adds a continual slow drip amount of muriatic acid into pool water. These may be used in salt water pools to mitigate the effect of high pH introduced by chlorine production.

> ➢ Always follow label directions to lower total alkalinity.
> ➢ One method, in the case of high pH is to turn off your pump to allow the water to settle, and add pH reducer/minus in one spot of the deep end of the pool. Keep the pool water still to burn off some alkalinity for 15-30 minutes.
> ➢ Bubbles may form and rise to the surface, this is carbon dioxide and is a product of the destruction of excess alkalinity.

> ➤ If your pH is normal, adding acid will reduce the pH and may cause further water balance issues.
> ➤ pH reducer should be diluted in a bucket of water before adding to the pool to prevent it from landing on the pool surface and etch or soften the pool finish.

The above method should be used only when the pH is high and your pool requires pH-reducer. If the pH is normal, adding a shock will reduce the pH to undesirable levels resulting in further pool problems.

pH – Acidity/Alkalinity – The water's pH level is the measure of its total acid-alkalinity balance. pH is important because it affects swimmers comfort, and proper balance protects the pool equipment.

pH is pronounced p H and written with a lowercase p followed by an uppercase H and stands for the power of hydrogen.

pH is a scale measuring the acidity or alkalinity of a solution.

The scientific definition is of pH is "the negative logarithm of the Hydrogen ion concentration."

In simple terms: pH indicates how acidic or basic the water is. pH should be tested daily at first. Once you gain experience with your pool, less frequent monitoring may be appropriate, depending on your pool's typical rate of pH change.

pH levels below 7.2 tend to make eyes sting or burn. PH below 6.8 can cause damage to metal parts, particularly pool heaters with copper heat exchange coils. High pH can lead to calcium scaling.

For lowering pH use either muriatic acid or dry acid. To raise pH use soda ash.

The pH scale runs from 0 (highly acidic) to 14 (highly alkaline). Distilled water, being neutral is pH 7.

The scale between 0 and 14 is logarithmic ... pH 8 is 10 times more alkaline than pH 7 and pH 9 is 100 times more alkaline than pH 7.

Ideal pH -   The ideal level for the pH of swimming pool water is between 7.2 and 7.8 per most manufacturer recommendations. We suggest you strive for a pH of 7.4 which is what your body will be most comfortable with since it matches your body's pH the closest.

pH is VERY important

The pH value is the chemical most affecting swimmer comfort.

It also affects the amount of hypochlorous acid (free available chlorine) that is formed, and impacts the sanitizing ability of your chlorine.

High pH

[85]High pH will cause cloudy water, staining, scale deposits (rough pool surfaces on all types of pools, filtration issues, and lessen your chlorine efficiency.

At a pH of near 8.0 calcium in water will combine with carbonates in the water, forming calcium carbonate or scale.

Calcium carbonate will form tiny particles and float suspended in the water, giving it a cloudy appearance.

High pH levels will make your eyes sting, and if ingested give you a sore throat. It may make your skin feel slippery.

Low PH

[86]Low pH will cause corrosion of pipes, etching of plaster, loss of chlorine levels, and irritation to swimmers, and itchy skin.

pH should be the most tested and watched chemical in your pool water, at the most frequent intervals, as it has the tendency to fluctuate the most,

---

[85] Corrosion and deposits on the inside of a salt generating cell. Cleaning with muriatic acid solution is needed

[86] The beginning of copper pipe corrosion in this heater component

and is the one that affects swimmers comfort the most.

Increasing and Decreasing pH

Always adjust your alkalinity prior to making your pH adjustment, as adjusting your alkalinity will often adjust your pH level as well.

Use a pH increaser or pH plus to increase your pH levels, use a pH minus/decreaser or muriatic acid to reduce your pH.

To lower the pH, muriatic acid must be added, pH minus is a granular/powder form of muriatic acid and often a bit easier to handle and store. Use caution and add a small amount of the acid to a full bucket of water before adding it to the deep end of the pool. The pool water should be circulating. Wait 6 hours and retest. Liquid muriatic acid can be added directly to the deep end of the pool. Take are in handling this, and add in small amounts so you don't overdo the change and end up having to adjust in the other direction.

To raise the pH, soda ash (sodium carbonate) must be added. When the pool water is below the recommended level of 80-120 ppm, you will need to add the soda to increase the alkalinity. The formula of 1 1/2 pounds of sodium carbonate will raise 10,000 gallons of pool water 10 ppm.

New Plaster or Pebbled Gunite Pools

Newly plastered or finished pools will have an unusually high pH for the first few weeks after installation. This is caused by a chemical reaction from the new finish, and you may have a hard time maintaining your pH during the curing period. This is also why it is important to hold off on adding salt to your pool during the first month after a new finish is installed.

CH – Calcium Hardness – Calcium hardness is the measure of the amount of dissolved calcium in your pool water. It is often referred to as the ability of water to lather with soap.

Just think of water that is run through a water softener, one drop of detergent will produce a lot more bubbles than traditional well or city water.

Calcium hardness lower than 100ppm makes water soft and will draw lime out of pool surfaces. Amounts higher than 400ppm, together with other chemicals may cause deposits to form on pool surfaces. Keep the calcium hardness in balance to prevent scaling and etching.

A combination of low pH, low alkalinity and low calcium hardness will cause water to become aggressive and leech minerals and metals out of the pool and equipment surfaces.

Causes of Hardness in Water

The two main elements of hardness in water are calcium and magnesium

Low Calcium Hardness

Pools with low calcium hardness levels will start to dissolve calcium out of the pool surface, whether pebble, plaster, tile, stone, concrete or even some fiberglass surfaces.

Prevent this from happening by keeping your calcium hardness levels at the proper level for your pool surface.

Foaming

In a spa, you want to keep your calcium at 150-200ppm to help prevent foaming.

A vinyl liner pool is less susceptible to issues in the pool surface from low calcium levels, however, low calcium hardness combined with low alkalinity and pH can cause damage to pool equipment, and especially a copper heater core.

Cobalt Spotting

127

[87]Calcium hardness helps fiberglass pools resist staining and cobalt spotting. Cobalt spotting is a condition related to the chemicals in fiberglass pools and spas, and appear as black or brown spots that won't brush off and will not be removed by algaecides or chlorine. Cobalt spots can often be removed by cobalt products specifically designed for this issue.

Adjusting Calcium Hardness

Calcium hardness is increased with calcium chloride.

> ➤ The best way to reduce calcium hardness is to drain some water and replace with fresh water (except if your fresh/source water is excessively high in calcium).
> ➤ Calcium hardness reducers can also be used. They contain chelating agents to bond with the calcium to keep it trapped in solution.

Low Calcium Hardness

Low calcium hardness can result in corrosive water.

In cases of low calcium hardness, especially in combination with low pH and alkalinity can lead to aggressive and corrosive water.

Your plaster, marcite, pebble surfaces, and grout will soften and can erode, etch, and metal equipment can oxidize, rust or leech metals into the water. This can lead to holes and leaks in heater cores, and staining of pool surfaces as metals deposit on the pool surface.

---

[87] Cobalt spotting on this gunite swimming pool with pebbled finish

This can be a cosmetic nuisance at the least, a functional issue for your pool equipment, and a noticeable rough surface issue at most.

High calcium hardness levels, in combination with high pH and alkalinity can contribute to scale forming on pool surfaces, in pipes, plumbing, and in your heater.

In cases of extreme calcium hardness, water will become dull and cloudy with the calcium precipitating out of solution.

High calcium levels can also irritate swimmers, causing sore eyes in particular.

Total Hardness

Total hardness in swimming pools is a measure of all the dissolved minerals such as calcium, magnesium and sodium.

CYA – Cyanuric Acid

Protects chlorine from being destroyed by the sun's ultraviolet rays. It is also often referred to as stabilizer or conditioner.

Stabilized Chlorine

Dissolving chlorine in water makes it unstable and subject to decomposition by ultra-violet light (the sun). Cyanuric acid will combine with free chlorine to help prevent decomposition by sunlight. We think of this as free chlorine is bouncing around in the pool, and can be zapped by sunlight. Cyanuric acid acts as inner tubes in the water that free chlorine can attach to, and when sunlight hits it, the inner tube keeps the free chlorine safe.

Some chlorine tablets are stabilized, meaning they contain CYA. In southern climates it is important to monitor the amount of CYA in your pool water to prevent high levels from building up. This is less of a concern in northern climates where pools will waste water during the closing process and keep CYA and TDS levels from building up over time. Too much CYA in water will lock your chlorine and render it ineffective - and not allow it to do its job. The higher your CYA level, the more free chlorine you will need to get the right sanitizing effect. Indoor pools will need much less CYA than outdoor pools exposed to direct sunlight.

Cyanuric acid is increased by adding a CYA product, stabilizer or conditioner to your pool, or it is introduced by the use of stabilized chlorine tablets.

> Stabilizer takes quite a while to dissolve, so add it slowly and avoid letting it settle on the pool surface. It will also increase your filter pressure as it is absorbed by the water, so account for this in your pressure readings.

> A good method for adding stabilizer to your pool is to put it in a sock and allow it to gradually dissolve into the water. Keep your pump running continually for 24 hours during after adding, and avoid backwashing your filter for a week (so add stabilizer after you backwash and balance your other chemicals).

> In almost all cases when you need to lower your CYA leaves you will want to drain and replace some of your water.

Take care not to drain too much during this process.

Salt - The salt level should be in line with the salt generator manufacturer directions. for the Pentair IntelliChlor units the recommended level is (3,000-3,500 ppm)

A note about: Salt Water Pools - when you are generating chlorine with a salt water system you may find that the pH tends to run high. Liquid chlorine has a pH of approx. 8. To offset this pH you may need to add pH reducer or muriatic acid to the pool. You can also keep the alkalinity on the low end of around 80ppm which should help the pH stay on the lower levels.

TDS or Total Dissolved Solids is the total of all the inorganic and organic soluble substances dissolved in the water. It is measured by assessing the electrical conductivity of the pool water.

Bottled mineral water usually has lower TDS levels than tap water.

Distilled or pure water has a TDS value of 0 ppm.

Drinking water can have a maximum TDS value of 500 ppm according to EPA Water Standards.

Swimming Pools should have a TDS level of 1500ppm or less.

Levels above 1500 ppm can lead to cloudy water, staining of the pool surface, the inability of water to absorb chemicals properly, scaling, hard water, and a salty taste.

Salt levels should be taken into account when determining TDS levels in salt water pools.

If the TDS level in your pool gets too high, the only way to remedy this is to remove some water and add fresh. Make sure to get the recommendation of your pool professional so you don't cause issue or damage to your pool.

There is no other way to reduce TDS effectively except to replace some or all of your swimming pool water.

88

---

[88] Vinyl Liner Swimming pool and Sheer Decent Waterfall by Legendary Escapes

Pool Water Problems - Metals

Common Culprits: Copper, Iron and Manganese

Copper

Copper may cause your water to discolor, though it may still appear clear.

If you have copper present in your water (this can be determined through a water test for copper), you can remove copper by adding a metal sequestering agent such as SeaKlear[xii] which will remove trace metals from pool water.

[89]If you have copper present in your water it will be important to determine where it came from. Possible causes are improper water chemistry damaging your copper heater core, causing metal corrosion and leeching into the water. If this is the case you will often find your heater core will begin leaking and need to be replaced.

[90]Copper may also be introduced by alternative sanitizing methods utilizing copper coils.

Copper can also come from copper based algaecides, so read labels carefully.

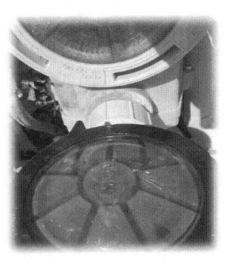

---

[89] Internal heater components showing some corrosion
[90] Can you tell this pool has well water?

Iron

[91]Iron is often introduced to water via your source water which may be high in iron content. If you fill your pool with source water which contains iron, and you have a sand filter, you can remove the iron through the use of FerriIron Tablets.

Manganese

Manganese is a mineral, and is often introduced to your pool via your source water as well. It may be present in the water, or leech in from pipes near manganese mining or processing operations.

Superchlorinating may oxidize manganese out of the water, allowing it to settle to the bottom of the pool where you could vacuum to waste to get it out of your pool.

As with iron, if you do vacuum to waste to remove settled minerals, you will lose water in your pool. If you are going to do this, it is best to overfill your pool, treat your water, and then vacuum, ending at the optimal level for your pool operation. Otherwise you're in a never ending cycle of adding water, vacuuming, adding water, treating, and so on.

SeaKlear is also a great resource for removing trace amounts of manganese from your pool water.

Green Hair

Green hair is often thought to be caused by chlorine, when really it is often the result of metals in the water that become deposited on hair. A product like Hair Renew by Natural

---

[91] Before and After, Iron Source Water and treatment with FerriIron Tablets

Chemistry, as well as specialized shampoos can help. If you have this issue, be diligent about checking for metals in your water to help prevent the issue in the first place.

Water Color Changes

[92]If your water changes color immediately after adding chlorine or another type of oxidizer, the pool water probably contains metal.

If you add liquid chlorine with a relatively high pH to pool water with iron, you will often notice an immediate change to a fluorescent green tinged water. This is because the higher pH introduced is pushing the iron out of solution and making it visible in water. The solution, if you have a sand filter, is to add FerriIron Tablets to sequester the iron, and allow the filter to filter the metal out.

Easy Identification of Metals

Green pool water = iron or copper

Brown pool water = iron (occasionally copper)

Purple/ black pool water = manganese

FerriIron Tablets are an excellent product for removing iron, manganese and trace minerals from the water, as well as SeaKlear.

Dealing With Metals

Iron, copper, manganese, and cobalt are metals which commonly cause colored water or stains in pools.

---

[92] FerriIron Tabs treat swimming pool water to remove the iron and allow sand filters to remove it from the pool

If you have fill water that is well balanced you will not have to deal with these metals.

If your source water is high in iron, you will need to use a product to remove the iron from your pool water. FerriIron Tablets are an excellent product for removing iron, manganese and trace minerals from the water, and work best with sand filters.

SeaKlear will also remove trace minerals from pool water (though it may not be enough to remove high amounts of iron from your water) and is safe to use in all types of pool filters.

Adding Chemicals

After you have performed your pool cleaning, and any filter cleaning or backwashing that is necessary, you may begin to add any chemicals needed for balancing.

When mixing chemicals with water, make sure to pour the chemical into a bucket that contains water, versus pouring water over any chemical.

Even if you skip over parts in this book (you'd never do that, would you?) be sure to READ your labels and instructions on any chemical you add to your pool.

Bromine

Bromine is another sanitizing agent that can be used for sanitizing pool or spa water.

It is more commonly used in spas, as a stable form that does well in hot water temperatures in spas which often have higher pH levels.

Chlorine is able to achieve better water clarity than bromine can.

People may be surprised to find out that bromine actually contains chlorine. Bromine in the solid form of bromochloro-5.5 dimethylhydantoin, contains 66% bromine, and 30% chlorine.

Pool Water Problems - Algae

Algae

[93]Some algae growth gives water a greenish tint, while black algae usually grows to produce individual spots. A chlorine shock will often remove algae, but if the problem persists, draining and scrubbing the pool with acid may be necessary. Algaecides are also used to fight algae.

Mustard Algae

Common algae in pools appears yellow-brown or "mustard" colored. Although it brushes off the walls of the pools easily, it quickly returns. It often grows in shady areas when there is poor water circulation. And , it resists chlorine and shock treatment.

[94]Solution: Use an algaecide along with chlorine shock. Follow label directions. Place all vacuum equipment – hose, head, pole, brushes, etc. into pool during treatment to get rid of as much of the algae as possible. Maintain a higher than normal chlorine reading for 4 to 5 days after the treatment.

Green Algae

Green algae is one of the most common problems for pools. It usually appears in

---

[93] Progress during a pool opening with an extremely algae covered pool
[94] Green Algae suspended in the swimming pool

corners or other areas where circulation is poor, though it can appear anywhere. Once established, green algae can grow quickly.

Solution: Use Algaecide along with chlorine shock. Follow label directions. It is also recommended to use a flocking agent, and always vacuum to waste or drain (do not backwash) so the dead matter can be removed completely from the pool.

Black Algae

[95]This is very resistant (stubborn) form of algae that clings to the pool's walls, floor, and especially into cracks. It especially likes gunite/concrete pools. The longer black algae are present, the longer it will take to get rid of it, so treat it as soon as you see it. Black  algae can pit the finish in a gunite pool.

Solution: Brush algae spots vigorously with a stiff algae brush and pour algaecide along the sides where spots are visible. Run filter continuously and shock the pool to eliminate the algae growth.

High powered algaecides such as Black Algaetrine® are best used in this case as well. Follow the label directions.

Preventing Algae

- ✓ Brush walls and pool floor weekly
- ✓ Vacuum pool weekly
- ✓ Use a maintenance dose of algaecide weekly
- ✓ Maintain a proper chlorine reading

---

[95] Black algae in the grout lines of this tile

✓ Keep your water chemistry balanced

Iron / Copper

[96]Depending on the oxidation state, it may cause your water to be green, brown, or red. Copper is blue or blue-green and manganese/iron is brown or black. If there is a large enough concentration, either will cause problems. Test kits are available to measure the presence of these metals.

Cloudy water may be caused by unbalanced water with a positive saturation index with either pH, hardness, and alkalinity, or even all being high.

Occasionally, high chloramine levels have caused cloudiness and high total dissolved solids can also be blamed for cloudy water. Filtration problems can also be a cause.

Chlorine odors and eye burn can usually be traced to high chloramine levels. Superchlorination will relieve this type of situation.

Treatment usually consists of chlorine shock or alum flocculation to remove these metals. There are also sequestering products available which will keep the metals bound in solution and prevent them from depositing and staining.

---

[96] Pool water with iron in the source water, high pH for a combination of suspended iron in solution. Treatment with Ferri Iron Tabs will remove the problem iron.

Common Water Problem Q&A

Green Water

Pool Turned Green After Adding Chlorine

If you shocked the pool and then it turned green I'd look at the pH being the culprit. If it is a fluorescent shade of green, that is a common indicator of high pH and high alkalinity.

[97]You can't get a good reading of alkalinity and pH when your chlorine level is high. So I'd test the water, see what the chlorine level is, if CL is over 3, you won't be able to read the others accurately. Let the chlorine level go down, and then adjust the rest of your levels according to what your test kit says.

One other possible cause of green is if you have well water/high iron content. Chlorine added to a pool in that situation can also cause the iron to come out of solution (i.e. be pushed out of the water) and also account for some discoloration. If that is the case, our FerriIron Tablets help remove iron from a pool that has a sand filter.

My Well Water Turned Green when I added Chlorine to My Pool

If you have well water what probably happened was the chlorine caused the pH to increase just enough to cause the

---

[97] Fluorescent green discolored water from high pH and iron in the source water

water to change color (high pH = fluorescent/lime green) – and then additional shock pushed any dissolved metals out of solution (iron = dull green/brown).

What I would do would be to add pH- to bring the alkalinity and pH down, followed by FerriTabs to take the metal out of the water.

Total Dissolved Solids - Run High

Pools do need to be drained and refilled, however only when your TDS (total dissolved solids) measurement gets too high. We'd estimate every 5-10 years for that. This is more common in southern climates where water evaporation will leave behind solids in the water, and the water is kept in the pool year round, versus the north where the pools are drained for closing and refilled for openings.

High Chlorine Demand and Stubborn Algae

Water chemistry if you leave the water in the pool:

The water chemistry – the reason you'd be doing through a lot of chlorine is because your conditioner or stabilizer level is probably low. The stabilizer acts as an "anchor" for the chlorine molecules. If you just pour chlorine in a pool as soon as sunlight hits it, poof, It's gone. If it has something to adhere to, the conditioner, then it can bounce around the pool until it is needed to be used. I would get your chemical levels tested at a pool place if possible where they can give you a digital reading. Get the TDS checked also. Then start with the conditioner, there is a great product on the market by Natural Chemistry called Instant Conditioner – that will get your conditioner level up quickly. The other conditioners/stabilizers come in a granular form and you usually put them in a sock for slow dissolving into your pool, either way is fine, but one is much faster. Conditioner should be between 30-60ppm. With the chlorine use you explain I'd think it's much lower.

The next step will then be to shock your pool with liquid chlorine. 1 case per 10,000 gallons is a good start. You can repeat the process every day until it clears up and you should be able to get rid of the algae. Other than a high chlorine reading for a few days, you could still swim (just be sure swimmers rinse off when exiting the pool). If you still have some algae, you can use a strong algae product such as algae crush. The other treatment for algae that won't go away is to treat with a phosphate remover, phosphates are the food source for the algae, so eliminate the food source, eliminate the algae.

Once those are under control, I would also make sure your alkalinity, pH, and calcium hardness are in the proper ranges. Treat them in that order. I'd wait until after shocking, as anything you do with the chlorine will cause some fluctuations in the pH level, so doing it after the algae treatment would make sense.

If you decide to drain and refill the pool (only do this under advisement!), once the pool is full check the range on all your levels. Make sure that you adjust the stabilizer as fresh water usually doesn't have any at all. Then adjust alkalinity, pH, and calcium hardness, and start maintaining with your chlorine as usual.

Closing Your Pool

[98]In southern climates it is common to leave a pool open, but have it in a more dormant state. In the north where cold and ice are expected, closing your pool is the best option.

Time the closing so it can be done before the first snow of the year. It is much better for your pool team to close your pool when the weather is warmer than colder. In extreme temperatures the plumbing pipes and valves can become brittle and easily broken during the process.

We recommend that you contract your local pool professionals to winterize your pool. It is something that can be done by a homeowner, if you know what you are doing and are very thorough. This is a case however, where paying for expertise pays off in the long run.

A pool closing uses antifreeze, which is specific to swimming pool plumbing. In a pinch you can use RV antifreeze. You should not use automotive antifreeze used in the radiator.

Handrails and Ladders are typically removed for the pool closing. They will get in the way of the pool cover if left in place. It is not necessary to remove the diving board (our team usually covers them with plastic), and leave the pool light in place. In the olden days (yes, we said olden days) it was common to remove the pool light and place it on the pool deck, or allow it to float in the pool. This is an antiquated process.

---

[98] Safety Covered Swimming Pool - Dipping like this is normal

The most essential part of a pool closing is to get your water out of the plumbing lines by blowing the lines out and adding antifreeze through the skimmer. If the lines aren't properly winterized any water trapped inside can freeze and expand, and crack your pipes over the winter. This can cause costly repairs if underground or if things break in in-opportune places.

If you winterize the pool yourself, make sure you know what you are doing.

Water Chemistry at Closing

A week before you plan to close your pool, perform your final water chemistry check and balance ALL of your chemicals. pH, Alkalinity, and Hardness levels all need to be in the proper range for your pool to not have scaling or etching issues over the winter. It is very important that ANY pool surface (concrete, gunite, shotcrete, vinyl-liner, or fiberglass) have balanced pool water while sitting idle all winter.

During the closing you will typically shock the pool (we suggest liquid be used for your closing of a vinyl liner pool) - there won't be any chance of granules settling to the bottom to possibly bleach a liner over the winter.

Final Routine Maintenance

[99]Keep your pool as clean as possible as you approach your pool closing, especially if you are hiring someone to complete your closing. We have seen too many cases of people neglecting or outright ignoring their pool in the month leading up to the pool closing. If you have excessive leaves and debris in the pool it will not only make your closing more costly, it will alter the water chemistry needs of your pool and possibly cause staining and issues over the winter.

Do a final brushing and vacuuming before winterizing the pool.

Draining the Pool

During a pool closing the water will need to be drained to below the returns for proper winterization. If you have a fiberglass pool, the water level is typically only lowered below the skimmer and either elbows with plugs or special plugs are used for winterizing your lines. It is important to keep as much water in your fiberglass pool as possible, and this process will allow that to be the case.

144

In the case of an automatic pool cover, it is also common to only lower the water to the bottom of the skimmer and use elbows or special plugs during the line blow out process. Some pools with automatic covers will also refill the pool to put the cover back on. A skimmer seal will often be used in this case.

To drain a pool:

- ✓ Turn the equipment "off."
- ✓ Move the skimmer valve(s) to the "closed" position so that ONLY the main drain valve is "open."
- ✓ Move the multi-port handle from "Filter" (or the current position) to "Backwash" or Waste" (or "Drain"). Putting the filter on backwash during this process will allow for a final cleanout of your filter and set you up for an easy spring opening.
- ✓ Turn the equipment back "on."
- ✓ The water will drain through the waste-line.
- ✓ Stay close until finished. You do not want the pump to run too long. Too little water can be harmful by allowing freeze and thaw cycles to move things you don't want moved. If you replace water with fresh, remember that it needs to be brought up to the right chemistry.

If you do not have a main drain, you will need to drain the pool with a submersible pump or create a siphon with your garden hose.

A pool professional will bring a heavy duty pump to get the pool drained quickly and to the right level.

100

What to Do While the Pool is Draining

These are items you can take care of while the water level is draining:

If you have a heater, make sure you turn off the power source to the heater, and close the gas line.

Remove your ladder, hand rails and move any deck equipment out of the way.

Get your cover ready. In the case of a safety cover you can lay out the cover first and screw the grommets up second. If you pull the anchors up first take care not to drag or snag the cover on any anchors during the cover install.

If you use a mesh safety cover, begin pulling up the anchors with your allen-wrench, or better yet, a (charged) cordless drill.

In the case of a plastic cover and water bags, get the cover ready to spread out (this is a typical two person job) and fill your water bags to 3/4 full to allow room for expansion during the winter freeze. If you use a water bag cover, begin filling the water bags (or hauling out the heavy sandbags). Remember that anything you use to hold down the cover could get swept

---

[100] A trash pump with 3" hoses for quick removal of water during pool openings and closings

into your pool during a VERY bad storm. Do not use anything that could harm, crack, slice, your pool surface.

Find your winter plugs, and gizzmos.

Once your pool Is Drained

- ✓ Once the water level is immediately below the lowest plumbing line necessary you should open your skimmer line slightly to make sure all water is out of that line.
- ✓ Next, turn off your equipment to stop draining the pool.
- ✓ Remove the "eyeballs" from the return jets
- ✓ Remove the skimmer basket(s) from the skimmer(s).
- ✓ Add your winterizing chemicals:
- ✓ We suggest liquid chlorine whenever possible for your pool shock at closing. When this is not possible, be sure to dissolve granular shock in a bucket until fully dissolved and add to the perimeter of the pool.
- ✓ Add a winterizing algaecide to the pool.
- ✓ A Winter Pill or stain/scaling preventative can be added at this time.

101

---

101 Final Cleaning of debris during a swimming pool closing

Blowing Water Out Of the Plumbing Lines

Step #1: ***call your local pool professionals.*** If you still insist on actually doing this alone, proceed to the next step. But we highly... OK, we've said it enough times.

What you will need:

- ✓ Antifreeze
- ✓ Plugs
- ✓ Skimmer "Gizzmo" or Plugs (an empty antifreeze bottle can be substituted for the "gizzmo" - it allows for expansion in the skimmer.
- ✓ Blower - strong enough to winterize your lines. We suggest a pool specific blower to be sure it has enough pressure to get the job done. If you don't own one, contact your local pool professionals and pay them to winterize your pool. (Oops, said it again.)

If you do have the right blower for the job, keep going. If not, please call and schedule your pool closing.

Remove your drain plugs from your pump, filter, heater, and any ancillary equipment.

Remove the lid from the pump housing, the front part of the pump.

Once the pump is empty, thread the pump drain plug(s) back in, temporarily.

Begin by blowing out each return line, and plug. Also blow out the skimmer, and blow some antifreeze through the line. Plug the skimmer and add a bottle of antifreeze to the skimmer reservoir. Place the empty bottle upside down in your skimmer if you are not using a gizzmo.

During your winterization process, remove the plugs from the heater. In older heater models you also need to disconnect the pressure switch. Make sure you gas valve is in the off position. Some heaters have a plug that is relatively hidden that should be removed to allow for any residual water to drain out during the winter. Refer to your heater service manual to identify if this is the case with yours.

If you have a salt system, you can leave the salt cell in place for the winter, or you can remove it and store inside.

If you have a chlorinator or chemical feeder, remove the plugs, remove any excess tablets. If the feeder is in line, return the cap. If you have an offline chlorinator, such as the CL220, you need to drain the chlorinator, and remove it from the system. Store this indoors. If you do not, the chlorinator may freeze and crack, and you'll need to replace it in the spring.

[102]*A good place to store all these miscellaneous parts is the pump basket within the pump housing*. Keep the lid on all winter long to protect these parts. This is where your pool professional will look first when opening your pool in the spring.

If you have completed all the items on this list, give yourself a high five. If you decide it's a little more work than it's worth, make sure your local pool service company is now on your speed dial.

---

[102] Store loose parts like plugs and pressure gauges in the drained pump basket after winterizing your equipment system

Installing a Safety Cover

[103]Safety covers are the best cover option for your swimming pool. They are something you should consider if you have an auto cover as well. The snow and ice load and seasonal conditions can take their toll on an automatic  cover and you can prolong the life of your automatic cover, and keep it functioning longer if you have a safety cover added for winter.

Here are the steps to installing your safety cover for the winter months:

With your allen wrench, or better yet, a cordless drill, pull up the heads of all of the anchors.

Unfold the cover so that you can see how it will fit over the pool. Be careful that you don't snag or drag the cover on any of the anchors if you pulled them up first. Alternatively, unroll the cover first and use buckets of water to hold the cover in place while you screw up the anchors and get ready to install. [104]

---

[103] Merlin Safety Cover installed by Ask the Pool Guy
[104] Merlin Safety cover with wire cable secured to this raised waterfall

Using your safety cover tool, install the springs to the anchors on one side of the pool.

If you have a rectangle pool, attach the springs to the anchors on a short side.

If you have any other shape of pool, attach the springs to the anchors on any strategic side in order to start. If you have a special safety cover that is wrapped around a spa or wired across a waterfall, start with those areas (or better yet have your pool professional do this for you). Walk the cover to the opposite side and, using your tool, attach the springs to these anchors.

105

Tighten the straps on any of the springs that have become lose. You want the cover to be stretched relatively tight during installation. The cover will dip with the snow load during the

105 Use the notched stainless steel tool provided with the cover to install and remove springs to anchor the cover in place for winter

151

winter months, and even when this happens you want to ensure that nothing can fit in between the cover and the pool, causing any type of entrapment issue.

Installing a Plastic/Water Bag Cover

106

Here are the steps to installing a water bag cover:

- ✓ Fill all of your water bags to about ¾ full of water. You need to leave a bit of space to allow for the expansion of freezing water.
- ✓ Unfold the cover so that you can see how it will fit over the pool.
- ✓ Place the water bags over the cover on one side of the pool.
- ✓ If you have a rectangle pool, place the water bags over the cover on a short side.
- ✓ If you have any other shape of pool, place the water bags over the cover on any strategic side in order to start.

---

106 Plastic Cover with Waterbags full after spring rains

- ✓ Walk the cover to the opposite side and anchor the cover with water bags on this opposite side, taking care not to allow the pool water over the top of the cover.
- ✓ Allow the excess cover to fit (droop) inside of the pool at water level, do not stretch it tight, as the cover needs to allow for seasonal rainwater and snow to settle on the cover. It's better to direct how this happens than to stretch the cover and wait to see what the seasonal load will do.
- ✓ Place water bags on top of the cover on the remaining sides of the pool. Fit them around the pool from end to end, not leaving any areas where wind could blow under the cover and displace it.
- ✓ Once your plastic the cover is on the pool you can add a little water to help weigh the cover down, or leave it secured and allow the future rain and snow to weigh it down for you.

If you have a plastic cover, now is a great time to get a quote for a safety cover for next year, and save up towards it. You will love a safety cover for so many reasons, safety and aesthetics included![107]

---

[107] Plastic Covered Pool = unsafe and unsightly

108

Winterizing Your Own Pool - Things to Consider

If you don't winterize pools for a living it would be really easy to overlook an important step. When in doubt, hire someone to do this for you.

All water has the potential to freeze. A pool closing helps to remove water from the critical places, and add antifreeze to others to protect your plumbing and equipment.

---

108 The same pool, with a safety cover and toddlers = safe and pretty!

Winterizing an Aboveground Pool

Many above ground pool owners will hire someone to winterize their pool.

If you do decide to winterize your above ground pool yourself, follow as many of the inground steps as your system permits such as cleaning the pool and balancing your water. From that point, follow your manufacturer's directions for winterizing your pool and equipment.

Once you have winterized your pool, if you are able to move your pump and filter inside for winter storage, please do.

This is not necessary, however it will reduce the chance of freezing and damage to your equipment.

109

---

¹⁰⁹ Above ground pool, plastic cover and water tubes

Equipment Primer

Types of Pool Covers

What's the difference between a regular pool cover and a safety cover?

A typical solid vinyl pool cover is little more than a tarp to put over your pool. Typically it is anchored with water bags or water tubes. The tubes are filled with water, which do freeze during the winter. It is common that tubes will leak or break during the winter months, so having a few extra on hand is a good idea. Some homeowners place bricks or large items on the cover to anchor it in the event of loss of the water bags. This is not ideal, especially since a large item sitting on the edge of the pool could fall in or be pushed in, and cause possible damage to the liner in a vinyl liner pool. During the freeze cycle of winter, the top section of water in the pool does freeze. If something were to disrupt the ice and shove it into the walls of the pool, there could be issues. In a vinyl liner pool ice could puncture the liner. Though we don't see this often because preventative measures are taken, it is a possibility.

The plastic pool cover does not prevent children or pets from gaining access to the pool.

All safety covers must conform to the Standard Performance Specification set by the American Society for Testing and Materials (ASTM). According to the ASTM, a safety cover must be able to support a certain amount of weight, not permit gaps that a child or pet could squeeze through, and remove standing water. They are also a lot better to look at over the winter months. A plastic tarp with stagnant water and leaves and debris is unsightly. A safety cover which looks like a trampoline stretched over the pool is a lot more aesthetically appealing.

While a plastic tarp does keep the majority of the leaves, debris and silt out of the pool, it is still possible for wind to sweep some in. Plastic tarps are also typically good for 2-4 seasons.

They can develop punctures, tears, and the weave can thin out, allowing the dirty top of the cover water to seep into the lower pool. If this happens, it is time to get a new cover.

The mesh safety cover is ideal because it will keep the pool area safe, debris out of the pool, (though some can also be pushed under the cover in high wind/highly landscaped areas), and will filter out most of the silt, though a good vacuum in the spring will help if any does get through. The other benefit to the safety covered pool is that the mesh allows the snow and rain to melt through the cover and into the pool, resulting in a pool that is full when openings come around.

Plastic Covers

Does your pool look like this?

[110]The pool cover used on this pool is a standard plastic cover with water-bags. Sometimes these covers are used with water boxes, (a little harder and cumbersome to use), and sometimes patio blocks are used. Please don't use patio blocks to anchor your cover. If they fall into the pool they can cause major problems.

Plastic covers are relatively inexpensive, and will protect your pool from debris, and fading over the winter months. As long as your plastic cover is in good condition, it will cover the pool and keep dirty water on top of the cover.

Plastic covers typically extend over the edge of the pool by at least 5' in each direction so that the cover will sit down into the pool and allow water to collect on the top over the winter.

If your pool cover develops holes or tears over the winter, you will need to determine how much the water underneath has

---

[110] Plastic Cover and Waterbags

been affected. Sometimes you can get the cover off with minimal seepage, other times your pool may mix the top of the cover and pool water resulting in additional cleaning with your opening.

Please note: if your pool cover falls in and your water is dirty DO NOT empty your entire pool without consulting with a pool professional. You can ruin your pool liner, a gunite or fiberglass can have pop out issues and it is generally a very bad idea to empty your pool. We (pool professionals) have strategies to deal with this type of situation.

Plastic Covers and Drawbacks

Plastic covers are not the best option available to you as a pool owner. A safety cover will give you peace of mind and a well protected pool. Plastic covers and water bags are the most affordable option, and sometimes chosen for that reason.

A plastic cover (think large plastic bag on your pool) is a potential hazard for animals and children. If you also consider that people want to be as economical as possible, the cover manufacturers have [111]also follow suit. The cover manufacturers have been making plastic covers more cheaply and as a result quality has declined. Some covers may only last only a season or two.

Water bags are used to weigh the pool cover around the edge of the pool. They should be laid out end to end, and only filled 3/4 of the way full during your pool closing to allow for freezing expansion of the water. It's often a good idea to fill a couple of extra bags with your closing so you have extra to move around in case you have any pop or fail during the winter. Keep in mind if you fill the water bags and you have a

---

[111] Plastic cover sans water, waterbags, and most leaves, ready for removal

slow leak in any, they'll drain before long, so those are best replaced.

Again, avoid add cinderblocks or patio stones around the pool to anchor the cover. As logical as this may be to you, it *is not a good idea.* Anything falling into your pool can cause damage to the pool surface (especially a vinyl liner pool) so the money you save by using these anchors might result in a much more expensive repair or even the replacement of your liner. You will still have to pump the water off the cover for the spring opening and need to refill the pool to operational levels for the season.

Safety Covers

A safety covered pool is typically mesh or solid. (We really recommend the mesh covers for many reasons - easier to use, no need to add water in the spring and more convenient.)

[112]The investment in a safety cover will typically be more than a plastic cover with water bags. Covers do come in several stock sizes and shapes, however any custom pool will need to be measured with a cover designed specifically to the shape of the pool. Homeowners often wonder if they can just overlap a large enough rectangle over the pool, but we don't recommend this. The safety covers are made with specific wear areas for steps and coping, so if you don't plan for this your safety cover can wear prematurely and you can develop holes from wear in the wrong places.

---

[112] Safety covers are made for custom shapes, this geometric pool needed a few cutouts to fit the pool and make it the safest option possible

Safety covers are designed to support a person on the cover to prevent falling in. They may be tempting to use as a trampoline, however it will wear the cover, add stress to the springs, and it is best to just look, and not run around on the cover. Advise teenagers in your house to avoid playing soccer on a safety cover, and especially on a frozen pool with a plastic cover - the damage to the pool walls, and surface are too great a risk. (Yes, speaking from personal experience.)

A great benefit of a safety cover is that the rain and melted snow and ice will seep through the cover. You will have a full pool, and no need to pump water off the pool in the spring.

Some homeowners wonder if the pool gets too full in the spring if they need to pump water off their pool cover, either safety or plastic. The answer is NO. Allow your pool professional to remove water as needed at your pool opening. Too many well meaning homeowners have either taken too much water out of the pool and caused floating liners and issues, or in extreme cases the pool to pop out of the ground. That is too expensive, just wait, or ask your pool professional to come and assess the situation with you if you fell action is needed.

[113]Using special tools, the crew (say hi to Rick!) will release the springs from the grommets that recess into the patio for summer.[114] Screw grommets or anchors down so they are flush with your patio *before* you move the cover so

---

[113] Rick is ready to remove the springs from the anchors during this pool opening.
[114] See Ask the Pool Guy on YouTube for how to videos of this step.

that you don't catch and snag the cover. Carefully pull the cover off the pool, and take it aside to be cleaned and left to dry, before rolling it up for storage. This can be done by one person, but it's a lot more fun with two. Note: Although can you put your safety cover on at any time, it is usually considered too cumbersome to take off (and back on) every time you wish to use the pool.

With either cover, once the water is drained and the cover is removed from the pool the cover can be rinsed with the hose, or simply spread out to dry and then rolled up.

Take care not to leave a cover on the lawn for more than a short time. The longer the cover is on the lawn, the higher the chance of burning your grass and causing a large dead spot. (again, personal experience). The good news is that grass grows quickly and typically the spot will go away within a short amount of time (relatively).

Your pool supply house will usually have a cover cleaner which you can also use to clean the cover. Once the cover is dry, it is ready to fold and store. We suggest storing them indoors away from the elements to preserve the life of the cover. Also, especially with safety covers take note: rodents and insects love to build nests in the covers and if they take up residence will usually chew through several layers during their stay. This can be costly to fix, so storing the cover inside the garage or basement, or a well protected storage shed is best. Totes and large garbage cans can typically accommodate the size, though they are not foolproof to keep the critters out (again, personal experience.)

115

Yes, there is a safety covered pool underneath the snow!

---

115 Pool hide and seek in Michigan - Michigan winter is winning

Automatic Pool Covers

Automatic Pool Covers can be a great way to keep your pool protected from the elements, and from un-scheduled use.

116

Quick Tip: Always use the pump on top of your auto cover to keep the water pumped off. This allows for easy access when you need to open the cover, and also lessens the weight load on your cover.

Also, keep your water level at normal operational level during the summer so the auto cover can "float" across the top of your pool.

When closing your pool with an auto cover, try to keep the water just below the skimmer and use elbows to blow out your

---

116 Automatic Pool Cover - the darker the cover color, the less dirt you will see

return lines, preserving the water in the pool as much as possible.

How it Works:

A vinyl fabric is run between a track on either side of the pool.

An aluminum roller is on one end, and that houses the cover and tension rope while the cover is in use.

One of the ends of the roller is attached to a motor, which makes it 'automatic'. Automatic covers tend to look and work better on rectangular shaped pools, they can be added to just about any shape pool with the proper planning prior to construction.

Benefits:

Automatic covers help prevent evaporation during the summer by trapping moisture under the vinyl cover.

Automatic covers, that are kept pumped off can be considered a more safe pool, preventing access for children or pets.

Automatic covers will prevent leaves and debris from entering your pool.

Issues:

Dirty Automatic Cover

Use a garden hose, brush, and cover cleaner, as well as your cover pump. Clean the cover off in sections by removing debris, scrubbing, rinsing, and pumping off excess water, rolling it back as you go.

To help prevent discoloration you may want to use a vinyl conditioner each year.

Cover Mis-Aligned or Rolling Back Crooked

If you have this issue, the cover will need adjustment. It could be as simple as tightening the cover on the roller or track, or it could need more involved re-alignment. Consult your manufacturer's recommendations.

Broken Parts

If you try to open or close the cover with too much weight of debris or water on top, it can cause tears and broken parts. Consult your manufacturer's recommendations for broken part repair.

Motor Hums

If your motor hums and won't move, you can have internal motor issues, or have triggered a safety override of your cover. A professional service call may be in order.

No power to Motor

Check your breaker and switch. Check the motor for a reset button. Consult your manufacturer's recommendations for broken part repair.

Pool Equipment Specifics

How a Swimming Pool Works

Your swimming pool will pull water in from the skimmer(s) and main drains, into the pump, up through the filter, into the heater, and out back to the pool through any additional elements such as a mineral system, UV, ozone, chlorinator or salt generator.

The pump is the mechanical/electrical component of the system, and is responsible for pushing the water throughout the entire system.

Your heater utilizes electricity and gas (natural gas or propane).

117

---

[117] Basic Pool Equipment System, prior to the switch to all electronic ignition heaters

A basic swimming pool system typically has two pipes that come up from the ground into the front of the pump. These pipes are coming from the skimmer and main drain.

The water travels into the pump, up through the pipe, and into the top unit which is the multi-port valve. It is called the multi-port because it has multiple ports where it can send the water anywhere from filter to backwash to recirculate.

On the multi-port valve you will find the pressure gauge where you can watch when the system is running to see the pressure of the flow through the system. There is also a sight glass on the valve, which is where you watch when you are backwashing the system to see how the water looks flowing through the pipes.

Once the water goes through the sand filter, the water travels into the heater, back out of the heater, through the IntelliChlor salt generating system, and back to the returns of the pool.

Running Your Pool System

To work properly, your pool system needs to filter the water, and your chemicals need to balance and sanitize your water.

Your pool system should run long enough to turn over your water 2 full cycles in any 24 hour period. For energy conservation some people set a timer to run the pool system for a shorter time each day. The minimum we suggest you run your system is 8-10 hours a day. Stagnant water is a problem, so keep the water moving.

Please note that systems with salt/chlorine generators, your system will only be making chlorine while your system is running, so run it 24 hours a day for the best most consistent release of chlorine into your pool.

Newer pool pumps have energy efficient options. They will run at lower RPM's to continue pushing water, at slower speeds for a reduction in energy costs. To determine your savings, check out the Pentair Residential Pool Pump Savings Calculator[xiii].

Reasons for 24/7 operation:

Chemicals rely on circulation and filtration. If water is stagnant, filtration will be by-passed, and water chemistry will suffer.

If your water chemistry becomes unbalanced, you may need to invest in more chemicals to bring the water back into balance.

Your skimmer can't skim if the system is not running and you may end up with more debris at the bottom of your pool, increasing your need to vacuum and clean the pool, as well as additional chemicals to handle the contaminants.

Chlorine generating salt systems are only producing chlorine when the system is running. In some large pools, the system will need to be run 24/7 to allow for the production of adequate amounts of chlorine.

Reasons for 8-10 hours/per day operation:

Save on electricity. Well, maybe. There are new multi-speed pumps on the market that use less electricity running on low for 24/7 than at a higher rate for a few hours.

Pumps and filters should be properly sized prior to installation by your pool professional.

The equipment that is installed on each pool is done so on a case-by-case basis. When sized properly, the pump should send the entire volume of the pool water through the filter within 8-10 hours.

If you have any issues with keeping your water clear and sparkly, run your filter longer, clean your filter (backwash), and as needed use a water clarifier.

You will need to run your system longer during hot temperatures, during rainy or stormy weather, and during times of high swimmer use.

Pool Pumps and Motors

Your pool pump is the part of your pool equipment that makes the water move through the system. Without proper circulation you'd end up with a green pond instead of a pool.

Take care that you don't sweep dirt and debris into your pool pump at the equipment pad. Leaves and airborne debris can clog the pump. It is also best to keep chemicals away from the pump.

Most pool pumps/motors are designed for 24/7 operation.

Pool pumps should only run when they have water running through them. Priming the pump is getting the water to fully fill the pipe and pump and eliminating the air. Most pumps are self-priming, meaning they can generate the water flow and eliminate the air in the system. Some older pumps may require you to manually prime the pump before turning it on.

Newer pumps are also air cooled, meaning if they run dry it is not as critical as the water cooled pumps, which require water flow to keep the motors cool.

Keep the area around your pool pump, heater and filter free of obstructions. Also be sure you have enough air flow around your equipment pad.

If you experience power loss during particularly cold/freezing weather you should remove the plugs from the pump and allow the water to drain so they do not freeze and crack.

Sizing Your Swimming Pool Pump

You will need the following information:

- ✓ Pool Volume
- ✓ Capacity
- ✓ Flow rate
- ✓ Total Dynamic Head

These four factors are the basis for determining the correct pool pump size. Keep in mind the pump works with all of your other equipment, your filter, heater, plumbing lines, skimmer, drain, and returns. All of these need to be considered in choosing the right pump to ensure the correct turnover[119] rate for proper filtration.

The industry standard for a swimming pool pump is to complete two complete turnovers in any 24 hour period.

How Swimming Pool Pumps Work

Water is draw into the pump from the main drain and skimmer.

Water enters the pump where the basket sits, and into the impeller. The impeller is a rotating part of the pump that is attached to the motor, and creates centrifugal force which forces the water out of the pump and into the multiport valve, and finally into the pool filter.

After the filter the water will typically travel through the filter, and then the salt cell or chlorinator (if present), and then through to the return lines, waterfalls, slides and ancillary water return areas to the pool.

Pump Basket

Your pump basket is at the front of your pump housing, and has a clear lid to view the water inside the pump.

The pump basket has a hole on the front to allow debris into the pump, and to capture it before getting into the pump impeller or the filter.

Be sure when servicing your pump you reset the basket completely, and make sure the basket is put back in the proper direction, with the hole (if present) facing the plumbing coming into the pump.

To clean your pump basket:

---

[119] The number of times a *pool's* contents can be filtered through its filtration equipment in a 24-hour period is the *turnover* rate of the *pool*

✓ Don't attempt to service your pool equipment until you turn the pump power off

✓ Depending on your pool plumbing and equipment location (especially if it is located above or below your pool water level) it may help you to close your main drain or skimmer valves before removing the pump lid to prevent water from flowing back down the pipes to the pool.

✓ Turn off return valve (only if equipment is lower level than pool).

✓ Remove the lid from the pump

✓ Take note of how the basket sits in the pump so you can put it back the way you found it.

✓ Empty the basket of debris.

✓ You may also clean the basket with a garden hose, or a quick tip from our service team is to grab a bucket and scoop some water from the pool, insert pump basket (this also works for your skimmer basket) and give it a good swish and swirl upside down. This should release the debris and give you a clean basket to reinsert.

✓ Remove the lid from the pump housing-the front part of the pump.

✓ Note how the basket fits into the pump (so that you can put it back in the same way) and remove it.

✓ Check the O-ring on to make sure it reseats properly, and is lubricated. A cracked or dry O-ring may allow air or water leaks. Use only a water based lubricant for this.

✓ Make sure your pump has water present. If you have trouble repriming your pump, often adding water to the pump and forcing some into the plumbing will help the process along.

✓ Replace the pump lid, and secure it back in place.

✓ RE-OPEN your valves if you closed them for pool service.

Turn the equipment back on. When the pump starts you should be able to see the water begin to enter the pump through the see through lid. It should reprime within a few minutes. If it does not, recheck the basket and o-ring or gasket to make sure it is in place and in good condition, and add water to your pump or pipes as mentioned above.

If the pump does not fully prime or move water as it should after a minute or two, you may need to re-prime and troubleshoot. Refer to the "Pump" section for more information.

Variable Speed Pumps

Most swimming pool owners would agree that their pool is a great addition to their home. Pools add value to a home, they are great for entertaining, and they provide homeowners with a place to relax and enjoy those hot summer months. However, the cost of running a swimming pool can be high.

The average swimming pool pump can use as much energy as all other home appliances combined. They can cost $1,000 per year or more to run! A new type of pump, though, solves this problem. Variable speed pumps can cut energy costs by up to 90%, operating on just pennies per day. Installing a variable speed pump can save a swimming pool owner up to $1,500 in utility costs every year.

Our favorite variable speed pump is the Pentair IntelliFlo®. These pumps use a unique, advanced motor technology that provides a base savings of 30%. IntelliFlo® uses a permanent magnet motor, like the ones used in hybrid cars, instead of a traditional induction motor. These types of motors are more energy efficient and will save you money right off the bat.

IntelliFlo® is a smart pump. It comes equipped with variable speed capability, digital controls, and proprietary software that allow custom programming of ideal pump speeds for the specific tasks of your swimming pool. The speed of the pump will automatically adjust for filtering, heating, cleaning—even spa jets, waterfalls, and more. Older, one-speed pumps come with an unchangeable preset speed. This speed is almost never the optimal speed for any of the tasks of a swimming pool. We all know from driving a car: slower speeds are more efficient.

When pump speeds are reduced by half, energy consumption is just one-eighth of what was previously used. Even "high efficiency" single-speed, two-speed, and multi-speed pumps that cannot be adjusted are substantially less efficient than a variable speed pump.

Another benefit of the IntelliFlo® pump? It is unbelievably quiet. The permanent magnet motor that gives you outstanding energy savings is also a totally enclosed fan cooled (TEFC) design. Because of this, and the slower operating speeds, IntelliFlo® is the quietest pump you can install. When running at a typical speed, you can barely hear the pump.

IntelliFlo® also has a longer trouble-free service life than conventional pumps. The advanced motor produces less heat and vibration, and the TEFC design protects against the threats of an outdoor environment. The pump features built-in diagnostics that detect and correct conditions that cause premature failure. This protects against overheating, freezing, and voltage irregularities.

Whether you're building a new swimming pool, need a new pump, or looking for a way to cut costs, a Pentair IntelliFlo® variable speed pump is a great idea. While a variable speed pump does cost a bit more up front, the pump will pay for itself in the first year of operation. It is a great way to save money on utilities and do your part to go green.

Pool Heater

The best way to keep your heater in good working order is to use it.

Heaters manufactured today are required to meet certain efficiency standards. Millivolt heaters were manufactured with standing pilot lights. Today's models are electronic ignition and do not have standing pilot lights. [120]

If you have an older heater, here are the steps to light the pilot.

To light the Pilot:

- ✓ Turn off switch for heater thermostat.
- ✓ Turn main gas valve to pilot position and depress the valve and hold down.
- ✓ Light the pilot by pressing the button (on many models) or by using a lighter to light the pilot at the end of the pilot assembly.
- ✓ You can locate the pilot by following the small tube that runs from the main gas valve to where the heaters burners are located. At the end of this tube is the pilot head. When the pilot lights, continue to hold the main gas valve down for one (1) minute.
- ✓ Switch the main gas valve to on position.
- ✓ Switch on thermostat and turn up heat.

---

[120] Pool heater burners and pilot assembly

Heater Troubleshooting

- ✓ If your heater does not turn on, always backwash your pool filter if you have a sand or DE filter.
- ✓ If you have an older model heater, check the pilot to see if it is on. Wind or breeze may blow pilot out.
- ✓ Check the gas valve, make sure it is on and gas pressure is available.
- ✓ Check the pressure switch. This is a part that may need to be replaced.

Heat Pumps

Heat pumps are becoming quite popular as a way to heat an in-ground swimming pool. In Michigan they are best if used as an ancillary heat source (in addition to the main gas heater), as a gas heater may be needed for early spring, late fall, and if there is a spa connected to the pool for quick heating times.

We asked our local Pentair Pool Representative, Ingo, to tell us a little bit more about heat pumps, and here are a few notes from that conversation:

Benefits of Heat Pumps

- ✓ Heat pumps are efficient ways to heat a pool. Gas versus electrical costs are substantial.
- ✓ Titanium heat exchanger assures chemically challenged people longer life.
- ✓ Works even when temps get into the 50's.
- ✓ Excellent choice when used in conjunction with an auto cover.
- ✓ Perfect match with a gas heater to "maintain" heat throughout summer.
- ✓ Longer warranties on both the exchanger and compressor.

Considerations:

- ✓ On the down side: Much higher upfront cost
- ✓ Large unit on the pad
- ✓ Tends to spew out quite a bit of condensation. Homeowners think unit is "leaking"
- ✓ Takes longer than gas heater to heat up on initial cycle
- ✓ Larger breaker (50 amp) needed

As far as heating a pool, heat pumps are all about expectations. Whereas a propane/gas heater can take a pool from 65 to 80 in about a day, a heat pump typically would be longer to do that same job. That said, once we get to temperature a heat pump would be more energy efficient. Again, married with an auto cover where we don't have a ton of heat loss overnight, a heat pump can be a great choice.

In-Floor Heating & Efficiency Systems

One of our favorite ways to heat and clean the pool is through the use of in-floor heating, cleaning and efficiency systems.

By using products from the two best companies in the in-floor market we have customized our own system that we feel is the best available.

We install a series of in-floor jets and cleaning heads from our BlueSquare[xiv] and Paramount manufacturers, large in-floor drains from Paramount, and the maintenance free valve system from BlueSquare we can heat the pool from the bottom, and even better, eliminate the need to vacuum your swimming pool. Pair this system up with a variable speed pump for energy efficiency – and you have a pool that is heating from the bottom, continually filtering your water at a minimal electricity expense, and cleaning your pool all at the same time.

The in-floor heating, cleaning and efficiency system should be planned and installed with your new pool construction. It is

176

also an option during major renovations of vinyl liner and gunite swimming pools.

In-floor cleaning systems have been marketed in many regions of the country to simply to sweep and clean the pool. We have found that in the Michigan climate, they are an efficiency system when installed, allowing the pool to heat from the bottom up, and the cleaning is a bonus of having this system.

Proper winterization is also key. Most companies are used to winterizing pools with a skimmer, main drain, three return lines, and a possible pool sweep line. In-Floor systems will have dozens of additional cleaning heads and plumbing that needs to be winterized as well.

In-Floor System benefits are:

- Heat the Pool From the Bottom
- Add Chemicals from the bottom (preventing immediate loss or burn off from the sun).
- Temperature consistency through the pool, no thermal layers of hot and cold.
- Faster heating
- Cleaning - heads pop up on a pre-determined basis to move debris to the main drain at the bottom of the deep end

In-Floor Cleaning System

In-Floor cleaning systems, as they are commonly referred to, have a valve system located at the equipment head and heads in the floors and walls of the pool.

As each head pops up in each zone, it's kind of like a sprinkler system, the zone pops up, the head turns and goes back down.

The next one it pops up it turns and it sweeps the pool clean, and it's typically going to clean 80 to 90% of the pool.

In-floor cleaning systems are all mechanical. They're not electrical. You have an electric pump that driving water through a mechanical system.

There may be a little area that needs brushing if there is a hard to get corner.

Variable Speed Pumps and In-Floor Efficiency Systems

The other huge advantage today is using a variable speed pump. Instead of your pump running for eight hours a day and shutting off, now we can run twenty-four hours a day at a lower rpm, keep that water moving at all times and sweeping and cleaning continually, all day and all night, and that is another part of that efficiency that's made in-floor that much more important.

In-Floor Cleaning System Valves

[121]Some of the in-floor valves are simple, they have a turbine that turns a set of gears that that mechanical valve just slowly turns from zone to zone.

Others are a little bit more involved, a little more intricate with a lot of little parts that shift. It goes from here and it shifts hard to the next zone, shifts hard to the next zone.

The advantage of that is it's stop, start, stop, start, stop, start. The difficulty with that is the flow through the system, because as soon as you stop and shift zones you back the system up and the pressure goes up, and the pressure goes down, and the pressure goes up.

---

[121] BlueSquare Q360 InFloor Cleaning Valve

Filter Systems

[122]The job of your swimming pool filter is to keep your pool water clear and clean.

All pool filters are manufactured to remove dirt, debris and organic matter introduced into your pool by the elements and swimmers. They also filter out bacteria and algae.

There are three main types of swimming pool filters: cartridge pool filters, diatomaceous earth pool filters, and sand pool filters. The goal of your filter is to maximize your filtration process. The larger your filter area, the less often you have to clean the filter. Another goal of your filter is to use the least amount of pump energy to achieve the needed flow and subsequent turnover rate. The lower the pump power needed

---

[122] A tyipcal Legendary Escapes equipment pad with a variety of valves for features, large sand filter, side mount multi-port, Q360 valve in the R2D2 configuration for pool closings, dual pumps, salt generator and Mastertemp heater.

179

to push your water, the lower your utility costs and higher your filter efficiency.

Multi-port Valves

[123]Multi-port valves are also called filter control valves, backwash valve, Vari-Flo™xv valve, or even just "the multi-port." Occasionally it is referred to as the "spinney" thing with the handle. They are situated between the pump and filter.

[124]The multiport does not have a power source. All the water is pushed through by the pump from the pool main drain and skimmers. Once it passes through the pump it enters the multiport, which has multiple ports that tell the water where to go.

From the multiport typically you have filter, waste, backwash, rinse,

---

[123] Ask the Pool Girl and the MultiPort Valve. NEVER turn the handle when the system is running!
[124] Basic Vinyl Liner Swimming Pool System - sand filter with top mount multi-port, salt cell, Pentair Heater

recirculate, winterize or closed options.

The job of the multi-port is to tell your water where you want it to go.

There are top mounted multi port valves (photo to the right), which are mounted on the top of your filter. Side mount multi ports are located on the side of your filter.

If you don't have a multiport (similar to what is pictured above) you may have a push pull valve. The push/pull valve gives you the option for filter or backwash on your sand pool filter. They are simpler valves but limit the choices you have in running your system. If you have a push/pull valve, please consider having a multiport installed, or if it is time a filter replacement with a new valve might be in order.

IMPORTANT: Always turn your system off, if you are going to move the handle on the multi-port valve. If you move the handle while the system is running, you can blow the spider gasket, which is on the inside, out of place with the force of the water in the system. So don't do that. Okay?

The picture on the right has a Side Mount Multi Port Valve. [125]

Identify the different functions and settings that are on your multi-port valve. The typical settings are listed below:

Filter Setting

This pulls in water from the pool, sends it through the filter, heater and chlorinator or salt cell, and then back into the pool.

---

[125] Side-Mount Multiport System

Backwash

This is used to flush out the filter by pushing the particles that are clogging up the filter, out through the waste hose. The backwash setting reverses the flow of the water. Instead of going in through the top of the filter and down through the sand, the water goes in through the bottom, pushing the water up through the sand, lifting debris off the top and pushing them out the waste hose.

Rinse

The rinse function reverses the flow back to normal filter flow, with one exception, it continues to put the water through the waste hose to clean out any leftover debris in your pipes. If you turn the water back on to filter, and your pool returns are showing a fine mist of dust /dirt/debris back into the pool either you didn't backwash long enough, you didn't rinse long enough, or something is broken.

If the filter becomes very clogged, may be necessary to rotate between the rinse and backwash settings on the multi-port valve, until the water runs clean.

Waste

Some multi-port valves also come with a waste setting. This setting takes the water directly to the drain, instead of putting it through the filter and back out into the pool. This can be much more convenient for pool owners. (See the section on vacuuming for more information.)

IMPORTANT: NEVER, ever, let the water level drop to or below the skimmer (or designated vacuum line) with the pump running and your skimmer lines open. Air will get into the system which will cause your pump to lose prime.

Re-Circulate

The re-circulate setting on your multi-port means the water will enter the multiport and bypass the filter, going right back into the pool. You can use this setting to troubleshoot filter issues (for example if your heater won't start because your filter needs to be backwashed, or even a sand change) it will also help your pump to prime more quickly in some cases since the water will need less force to get through your system.

Multi-port Valve Maintenance

The handle on your multi-port valve should move freely when you move it. As a reminder: NEVER attempt to move the handle while your pump is running. The water pressure can break internal parts, or move the spider gasket. The spider gasket is located inside the multiport valve and seals the top and bottom of the valve together. If the gasket is out of place it can misdirect water, or allow water to leak through to locations other than where you want it to go.

The mulit-port is relatively simple to take apart and realign, however, avoid the need for this by operating your multi-port properly.

Your multiport valve should not make noise, or leak air or water during operation. The multiport valve usually has a plug, a pressure gauge and a sight glass. These parts will be taken off during your pool closing process, and re-installed at the pool opening. If you have a water or air leak in any of these areas, add some Teflon tape on the threads or magic lube and reseat. A drip that is infrequent is okay, anything more should be looked at.

The Pressure Gauge

The pressure gauge will indicate the pressure in psi that the your system is operating at. The pressure is the amount of force it takes the pump to push the water through your filter.

If the pressure on your pressure gauge is increasing, such as going from a normal operating pressure to a higher number, it means that it is taking more force to get the water through your filter. When the pressure increases by 5-7psi it is time for some maintenance. At this point clean your filter by backwashing in the case of a sand or DE filter, rinse your cartridge filter, empty your skimmer and pump baskets to make sure there is no debris impeding the flow of water.

If the pressure on your pressure gauge decreases, it may mean there is an obstruction in the flow of water, either in your skimmers, on the main drain, in the plumbing lines, or in the pump basket. Check all of these areas to remove any debris or objects (pool toys are often a culprit) that may be in the way.

If cleaning these areas does not solve the problem, you may have an obstruction in the plumbing, such as acorns, small pool toys or other objects that may become lodged in the pluming. Call a pool professional for help in troubleshooting issues like this.

If the pressure on your Pressure Gauge is DECREASING, you have an obstruction, which is typically a full skimmer and/or pump baskets. If cleaning all the baskets does not resolve the problem, there may be an obstruction in the plumbing, for this, it is best to call your local pool professional.

126

126 Pressure Gauge on a Sand Filter with Side mount multi-port

Sand Filter

Sand Swimming Pool Filters

Sand pool filters are our first choice for filters in the Michigan climate.

127

They are pretty easy to operate, and require just a bit of maintenance.

Sand filters are the Pool Guy's first choice for most Michigan pools, and for high iron content areas because they allow for the use of Ferrilron Tabs, a product that will help the filter remove iron from swimming pool water. Pool water is routed through the filter which is filled per the manufacturer's directions with sand.

---

[127] Swimming Pool Equipment Pad with Side mount Sand Filter

The water is forced through the filter from the top, through the bed of sand which filters out the contaminants, and into laterals (often called fingers) at the bottom of the filter.

The water is then sent through the laterals, up through a center tube, and back into the multiport valve where it then travels through the heater and any chlorinator or chlorine generator installed on your equipment pad.

Over time, dirt and debris will accumulate between the sand particles, and often in layers on top of the bed of sand. This is what causes the pressure in the filter to increase as it becomes harder for the water to pass through. This is the signal to backwash which will reverse the flow of water through the filter and send the dirt and debris out the backwash line.

[128]Sand filters are known to filter out particles as small as 20 microns.

129

---

[128] A peek inside this sand filter
[129] Sand inside the filter during a sand change, notice the debris on the top layer

Glass Filter Media

As of the time of this printing, there are also new glass media becoming popular on the market which creates more surface area in the filter for increased filtration to 4-5 microns. Activate by Maytronics is one of the new filter media available. It is made from recycled glass that goes through a special process of decontamination, sterilization, shaping and activation. This media will attract and capture bacteria and algae, and aid in the prevention of biofilm[xvi]. Activate will lower chemical consumption and has a lifetime guarantee - which we expect will decrease the need for a future sand change.

How to Backwash

When you notice the water circulation in your pool has decreased, and/or your pressure on your filter indicates an increase in pressure of 5-7psi above your normal operating pressure it is time to backwash.

Here are the steps:

- ✓ Turn your equipment OFF - this is very important, never attempt to turn the multiport handle while the pool is running.
- ✓ Turn the multiport handle from filter to backwash.
- ✓ Turn the equipment on.
- ✓ [130]Watch your sight glass during this process. The water will be cloudy/dirty in the sight glass. After it runs clear the backwash is finished. This commonly takes 2-3 minutes. If you stop the backwash too early, you may see debris blow back into the pool when you put it back on filter. This indicates you should

---

[130] Sight Glass

backwash, or rinse longer.

✓ The backwash process is wasting water from your pool system, so always check your water level before and after backwashing to make sure you are maintaining the proper amount of water in your pool.

Also, it should be pretty obvious that you should not add chemicals just before a backwash, or they may just end up going down the drain.

✓ When you are satisfied your sight glass is running clear, turn off the equipment.
✓ Rotate your multiport handle from backwash to rinse. If you have a push pull valve, at this point you would reset the valve to normal operation (as you cannot complete a rinse cycle). Rinse is important because it will eliminate dirt and debris from the multiport valve, and the filter internally to allow a clear path for your water to filter through.
✓ A rinse should take 30 seconds or so. Again, watch your sight glass during this process and stop when the sight glass runs clear.
✓ Turn the equipment off, and move the multiport handle from rinse back to filter.
✓ Turn the equipment on and resume normal operation.

131

---

131 Backwash/Discharge hose

Sand Changes

With normal operation, sand should be replaced every 3-5 years, or as you notice the filter needs more frequent backwashing, you have trouble keeping your chemicals balanced, you have more frequent algae formation, or if your water is dull and not as clear and sparkly as it should be.

This is something you can attempt yourself, however it is not a fun job. Many people who change their sand themselves the first time claim they will never again attempt it.

[132]A great time to change the sand is during your pool opening when the sand has had a chance to dry out in the filter over the winter. Scooping and vacuuming out dry sand is a lot easier than mucking wet sand out of a typically very small opening in the top of your filter.

During a sand change the laterals in the bottom of the filter should be checked for cracks and damage. If even one lateral has a crack or fracture sand can enter the plumbing and end up at the bottom of your pool.

---

[132] Inside a sand filter with cake like debris on the top layer of sand

When it is time for your sand change , you may want to consider a switch to an alternative media, such as the glass media mentioned previously. This will result in increased filtration and decreased need for maintenance of your sand filter.

Sand filters that are left without proper maintenance can develop several issues over time. Debris can settle on top of the bed of sand and form a barrier for the water to pass through effectively.

If water can't pass through the bed of sand it will often find another route, and will channel through the bed of sand, forming channels where water moves through without going through the sand as a filter. The water may also bypass the bed of sand and move down the sides of the filter, channeling that way instead. Both of these mean that your water is not being filtered properly, or able to remove the contaminants as it should.

If your water chemistry is incorrect, often with a high pH level, calcium and minerals will come out of solution in the water, and become trapped in the filter. As these combine with contaminants such as lint, hair and other debris, it can form a cake like substance which can block the filter. The calcium and minerals may also calcify into a hard block, or scale and cause deposits to form.

The solutions to all of these issues is to regularly maintain your filter, and watch for the signs that you may be in need of a sand change.

Diatomaceous Earth (D.E.) Pool Filters

[133]Diatomaceous earth (D.E.) pool filter results filter to a particle size as small as 3–5 microns. Small particles (40 microns) can't be seen with the eye, large quantities of small particles can have an effect on water clarity, which is the main reason to use a D.E. filter. With the new glass media available for sand filters, this is creating a new choice for the filtration previously only offered by a D.E. filter.

Backwashing - Cleaning a DE Filter

A D.E. filter will need to be backwashed when the pressure increases to 8-10 psi above the standard operating pressure.

[134]During the backwashing process in a D.E. the dirt and debris are removed from the filter. The DE powder is also removed from the filter during this process and needs to be replenished each time you backwash.

Some DE Filters have a bump mode in order to prolong the filter cycle and reduce the need to backwash by loosening the DE from the grids and allowing it to remain in the filter to recoat the grids and continue filtering.

---

[133] Inside a DE Filter
[134] Algae covered DE Grids in need of cleaning

Even with a bump feature, backwashing will eventually be necessary, as well as filter cleaning.

135

To Backwash your DE Filter:

When you notice the water circulation in your pool has decreased, and/or your pressure on your filter indicates an increase in pressure of 5-7psi above your normal operating pressure it is time to backwash.

Here are the steps:

- ✓ Turn your equipment OFF - this is very important, never attempt to turn the multiport handle while the pool is running.
- ✓ Turn the multiport handle from filter to backwash.
- ✓ Turn the equipment on.
- ✓ Watch your sight glass during this process. The water will be cloudy/dirty in the sight glass. After it runs clear the backwash is finished. This commonly takes 2-3 minutes. If you stop the backwash too early, you may see debris blow back into the pool when you put it back

on filter. This indicates you should backwash, or rinse longer.

✓ The backwash process is wasting water from your pool system, so always check your water level before and after backwashing to make sure you are maintaining the proper amount of water in your pool.

Also, it should be pretty obvious that you should not add chemicals just before a backwash, or they may just end up going down the drain.

✓ When you are satisfied your sight glass is running clear, turn off the equipment.

✓ Turn the equipment on and resume normal operation. At this point you will need to add new DE powder into your system through the skimmer per your manufacturer's directions.

✓ The DE powder will enter the filter and disperse over the DE grids to give you a new *filter cake* on the grids. (DE Filter – cake is good. Sand Filter – cake is bad. Mom's cake is the best!)

✓ Check your pool water chemistry and your water level after a backwash. Make sure your water level is at 1/2 to 3/4 the way up the skimmer. Then check the water chemistry.

136

---

136 This DE filter hasn't been cleaned or serviced in a long time, rendering the filtration process virtually non-existent due to the cake of DE in the canister

Bumping your DE Filter

When your pressure is above your standard operating pressure, turn your equipment off and utilize the bumping handle to slowly push down and quickly push up on the handle 5-10 times. This will allow the DE powder to release from the DE grids and fall inside the filter.

After you have completed your bumps, turn the equipment back on and the DE will resettle on your filter grids.

 the handle 5 to 10 times, DE powder will fall to the bottom of the filter.

If your filter the regenerative type, but you do not have a handle, you can gently hit the filter tank with a rubber mallet 5 to 10 times (carefully!).

Too Much DE

Too much DE powder can cause the filter cake to be too thick. If this happens the grids may compress against each other and cause the DE to clump on the grids. If this is the case, the filter should be taken apart and the DE filter cleaned with a good rinse and cleaning with a solution of muriatic acid and water, making sure not to tear or damage the grids. Your pool professional would be happy to do this for you.

Too little DE

Too Little DE powder can allow dirt and debris to embed on the grids, or conversely not attach to the grids at all and travel back into your pool. Just like Goldilocks, it can't be too little, or too much. It must be just right (refer to your manufacturer's recommendations).

DE Grids

It is a great idea to check the DE grids inside your filter, at least seasonally. Cleaning the grids should also be done as needed, or on a routine maintenance schedule. If your grids are torn or frayed, they will need to be replaced.

137

---

[137] Old torn DE grids from a high iron content area side by side with the new replacement grids

Cartridge Swimming Pool Filters

Cartridge filters are known to filter to the greatest degree of filtration, as small as 25-100 microns (particles smaller than 40 microns cannot be seen by the human eye). Taking care of your cartridge filter is also relatively simple. The filter should be cleaned once a season, or as your water clarity or water flow calls for. If the cartridge becomes clogged or work it should be replaced. A cartridge filter however may not be best in areas with high iron in the source water.

Cleaning A Cartridge Filter

[138]To clean your cartridge filter, the individual filter elements will need to be removed from the filter and cleaned with a garden hose or pressurized nozzle. There is no backwashing with a cartridge filter.

To clean your filter, turn the equipment off, and remove the lid to the filter tank. You may find that introducing air into the filter by removing the plug, or pressure relief valve will allow you to remove the lid more easily.

Many cartridge filters have a band around the center that needs to be loosened to remove the lid from the base.

Nothing during this process should be forced. If you have trouble removing your lid, or cleaning your cartridges, please call your pool professional for advice.

---

[138] a look inside the cartridge filter

Remove the cartridges from the filter. Some filters have one large filter element, others may have several smaller filters grouped together. Spray each with a garden hose or pressurized nozzle. Once you are satisfied they are clean, you can replace them back in the filter. Now is a great time to check the o-ring that is between the top and bottom of the filter. Lubricate this o-ring with a water based lubricant such as Magic Lube to create a tight seal, and extend the life of your o-ring. If you o-ring shows signs of wear, tears or frays, purchase a new o-ring for replacement. Note: these are not one size fits all, you will need the make and model of your filter to obtain the proper replacement part.

Put the lid back on and tighten, and resume normal pool operation.

Replacing Filter Elements:

Filter cartridges or elements should be replaced as needed, and per your manufacturer instructions. Some are recommended to be replaced early. In places with water chemistry such as iron that will clog filters quickly, more frequent replacement may be needed (or in some cases, like Michigan, consider a switch to a sand filter.)

139

---

[139] Old and worn cartridge filters, time to replace

Cleaning Filter Elements

Using a cartridge cleaning product may prolong the life of your cartridge filter. If you clean your filter elements and notice that they are cracked or torn, or the cleaning process tears them, it is time to replace.

Water Conservation

Many jurisdictions where water conservation is required may require the use of a cartridge filter because it seems that it would use the least amount of water (no backwashing). What these jurisdictions fail to realize is the rinsing process will also waste water during the process.

Pool Landscaping

Landscaping is one of the final touches with a backyard pool environment that we absolutely love. Great landscaping can make an incredible backyard experience even better. It helps to finish off the look and feel of the pool area, making it look polished and beautiful.

Pool landscaping is different from other types of landscaping, though, for several reasons. It is important to hire a landscaper who is familiar with swimming pools and the unique requirements associated with them.

140

Our resident landscaper, Jodi[xvii], gave some thoughts about pool landscaping.

Essentially, she says, you are creating a new environment with specific criteria for plant material.

Different types of landscaping have different requirements-- whether the landscaping is going in near a home, in the middle of a lawn, with cement, near a pool, etc.

---

140 Landscaping by NaturallyJodi!

The poolside environment has specific criteria when it comes to the plants that can be used. This doesn't have to mean you are limited or restricted in plant choice, but, if you have a landscaper who is not familiar with the various types of plant matter, you could find yourself with limited options. It's important to find a landscaper who is familiar with all the options for plant material so you have the widest variety of options available.

141

Poolside landscaping can be tricky--you want it to enhance, not overshadow, the pool!

Your typical, commonly-used plants might not be the best options for use near a swimming pool. Your landscaper should be conscientious about the specific requirements of a swimming pool environment. The most important thing to keep in mind is the fact that pools have working parts that can easily get plugged up without proper care.

Plants that drop a lot of leaves or other debris are not good poolside options. With the wrong choice of plants, you could be

---

141 Landscaping can give pools a feel from around the world. This pool features a Southwestern arid feel and the landscaping enhances the theme

constantly skimming debris off the top of your pool and vacuuming the water--and if you're not careful, that debris can get sucked into the skimmer and fill up your skimmer basket and pump basket, which can make your pool run less effectively and eventually damage your equipment.

Another important thing to consider when finding a landscaper for your swimming pool area is the goal of the landscaping. Most landscapers work to make the landscaping the focal point of the yard--this is understandable, as this is generally the reason they are hired. However, when it comes to pool landscaping, the focus should remain on the pool. Especially if you are building a unique or custom swimming pool, you will want the unique aspects and details of your swimming pool to shine, and to take center stage in the backyard. Landscaping designed to be the focal point of the yard will compete for attention, often making the yard look too busy or overwhelming. It is important to find a landscaper who respects the fact that the pool is the focal point, and will create a beautiful landscape design to accentuate and support your pool.

Zen Gardens

142

---

142 Zen Garden by Naturally Jodi

The Japanese rock garden (dry landscape garden or Zen garden) create a miniature stylized landscape through a carefully and thoughtfully selected arrangement of rocks, water features, moss, pruned trees, bushed, and sand. The sand is raked to represent ripples in water.

The sand is essential to the rock garden; however, you can also use small pebbles. In the Japanese Shinto religion white sand was used to symbolize purity. For Zen gardens, it represents water, emptiness, and distance. These are all places you seek to be through meditation.

Typically Zen gardens are small. They are usually surrounded by a wall and meant to be viewed while seated from a single viewpoint somewhere outside the garden. An ideal location would be a porch or small backyard area, or small area near your pool.

In modern-day pool and spa design, Zen gardens have grown in popularity. Not only are they calming and can help bring one's mind to peace- they are attractive. They look beautiful with most pool and spa designs and can be a great talking piece for guests or during backyard pool parties.

Landscape Do's and Don'ts

Mulch

Keep in mind with mulch next to the pool, if it rains, the wind blows, or somebody runs over it may get kicked or pushed into the pool. Depending on how it is made and colored, it could cause blockages in your pool pump/basket, and if it has dyes, they may stain your pool surface.

143

---

143 Landscaping bed with Mulch just outside the pool fence

River Rock

A large kind of river rock is a great choice for around a pool.

144

Slate Stones

Large and flat stones can be used around a pool. They are not likely to move much, and should be pretty safe.

145

---

144 Hybrid Swimming pool by Legendary Escapes with Landscaping and River Rock by Naturally Jodi
145 Landscaping beds with slate stone, great for a pool surround

Lava Rock or Popcorn Rock

146

One product absolutely to stay away from around the pool is the lighter lava rock, or it's called popcorn-type rock. It's really light. They can dye it a whole bunch of different colors so it looks great, but the challenge with that is it is so light that it blows into the pool.

If you get it into your skimmer basket and it makes its way into the pump, one of the things that those little popcorn pieces do is they jumble around in there until they get smaller. When they get smaller, they break into smaller pieces that can get through the slots of the basket. Often they get into the impeller of your pump and it crunches in there. We've seen a lot of pool pumps over the years that have fallen victim to this popcorn condition. If you have a choice, stick with something that's larger, that's not going to go through and cause issues.

---

146 Lava Rock - a Light weight and small loose stone not ideal for swimming pool landscaping areas

Landscape Lighting

Traditional Swimming Pool Landscape Lighting

Lighting around your pool can make all the difference to the enjoyment of your backyard pool. Most traditional "landscape lighting" packages include low fixtures that illuminate only the ground. They don't create enough light to enjoy the space. They are often capped at a height of under 2′ tall, shining on paths or up to light trees and walls.

A Legendary Lighting experience actually feels like the lighting was done on purpose for the people enjoying the space.

147

---

147 Legendary Lighting Package

Landscape Lighting Fixtures as Design Elements

Creating useable space with ambient light that is pretty and functional all the time is a key element of the Legendary Lighting philosophy. The fixtures become design elements during the day, and appear artful and eye pleasing. The lighting benefit is viewed at night, as they create the lighting experience that completes the environment, bathing it in warm, inviting light.

148

---

[148] Zen Screens create privacy from the lake and the neighbors on this Legendary Escapes Pool

Benefits of Low-Voltage Landscape Lighting

A few of the benefits of Low-Voltage fixtures used in pool lighting, yard lighting, waterscape lighting and entertaining area lighting are:

- ✓ ease of installation
- ✓ ease of moving the lighting elements
- ✓ can be installed near water
- ✓ use less energy than traditional lighting
- ✓ wires can be covered by light ground cover, no need for trenching
- ✓ dimmer than regular high-voltage fixtures

149

Photo Credit Aftab

---

[149] Useful night time lighting creates a great outdoor entertaining area!

Any high voltage lighting fixture can be converted into a low voltage fixture.

Some of our favorite Legendary Lighting Experiences have been created through creative re-purposing of non-traditional fixtures. Just think of lighting as art, and installing lighting with any object that can be illuminated.

150

---

[150] Legendary Lighting in the Pool House with unique lighting fixtures

209

Fences, Gates and Door Alarms

Every swimming pool needs a fence that will pass the local code for safety.

[151]Every state and city has different codes about pool fences gates and door alarms. Most of these rules and regulations are the same overall. Most mandate that all doors providing direct access from the residence to a new

swimming pool and / or spa be provided with door exit alarms or self-closing and self-latching devices, unless the pool and / or spa is provided with an approved safety cover or the pool and / or spa is isolated from direct access to the home by an approved pool fence and gate enclosure.

Swimming Pool Fence

Swimming pool fence must be at least 48″ High, with slats no larger than 4″ wide, and no more than 4″ from the bottom edge of the fence to the ground.

[152]

---

[151] Black Steel Pool Fence
[152] Measuring a gap in excess of 4" at the bottom of this fence, more stone will solve the issue

Swimming Pool Gates

The gates must be self closing and self latching. All doors from the home that are within the gated area must also have door alarms installed to pass the inspections.

153

If the self-closing and self- latching door/ gate option is utilized:

- ✓ The release mechanism for the self-latching device shall be placed no lower than 54 inches above the floor.
- ✓ The self-closing device must cause the door to close and latch automatically, without any other assistance.

---

153 Self Closing/Self Latching gate with Magna Latch

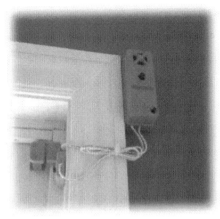

154

If the door exit alarm option is utilized:

- ✓ The alarm must be listed by Underwriters Laboratories (UL) as an exit alarm.
- ✓ The alarm must sound an audible, continuous warning when the door is opened or left ajar.
- ✓ The alarm deactivation mechanism must be mounted at least 54 inches above the floor.
- ✓ The alarm may be battery operated or may be connected to the buildings electrical wiring.

155

[154] YardGuard Door and Gate Alarm
[155] Pool Guard Door and Gate Alarm

212

Swimming Pool Renovation

[156]Gunite Swimming Pool Renovation

A traditional gunite swimming pool renovation will typically include work on the tile, coping, patio, skimmer, and the pool surface itself such as marcite or pebble.

---

[156] Kaylee removes tile during this gunite to vinyl liner pool conversion renovation

157

Painted Gunite Swimming Pools

If a gunite swimming pool has been painted, typically the pool will need to be re-painted every 1-2 years. If you haven't already painted your gunite pool, we recommend that you do not. It's relatively simple to acid wash a gunite pool surface, whether marcite or pebble, but once you put paint on the surface it is not a great option. The only way to return a painted gunite pool to its best condition would be to sand blast the paint off the surface and perform a re-marcite or re-pebble process.

Gunite Swimming Pool Main Drains

When a gunite pool is being re-surfaced, it is also a great time to perform a main drain update. Many older gunite pools are equipped with just one main drain. The code currently requires two dome-shaped drains, spaced at least 5' apart be installed on new installations. At the least the main drain should be

---

[157] Newly formed sun ledge on a concrete wall vinyl liner pool renovation

changed to reflect the dome-shape, and wherever possible, updating to two is the best choice.

Gunite Swimming Pool Skimmers

Gunite pools also often experience leaks at the skimmer, and cracking in the skimmer itself. This is due to the shifting of the ground for a variety of reasons, including seasonal freeze/thaws, and overall ground movement. It is very common to see pool putty in a gunite skimmer that helps to patch any leaking areas to try to avoid having to replace the skimmer entirely.

158

A skimmer replacement can happen at any time, and would include cutting the concrete or patio to expose a foot or two of work space surrounding the skimmer. The skimmer is then dug out, removed from the pool deck, and the pool, and a new one installed. There may be some damage to the tile or surface of the gunite pool, no matter how careful the process may be, so some patching and repair work of the marcite, pebble and tile may also need to be done.

---

158 Gunite skimmer assembly

215

Gunite Pool Tile and Coping Replacement

It is possible to perform a renovation and replace the tile at the waterline of the pool. Keep in mind if you would also like to renovate or replace the coping, this should be done at the same time as the tile since the removal of the coping stones could cause tile to fall off and it is best to plan ahead.

159

The definition of coping is the cap on the edge of a swimming pool or spa, which is mounted on the bond beam.

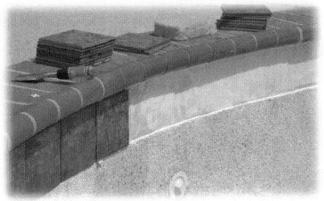

160

---

[159] Gunite pool with missing tile, time for a tile replacement of the entire pool. Doing just a part is not a long term fix as tiles falling are like Dominos, once one goes...

The function of Swimming Pool Tile

Tile on a swimming pool performs the functional purpose of disguising the scum line or "bathtub ring" that would be visible on the surface of the pool due to the fluctuating water line due to evaporation, swimmer load, and water level.

Many homeowners may wonder if eliminating the tile line would be a better option, especially in climate where freeze/thaw and beam shear may be a concern. The tile is really the best option for the top edge of the pool, as it hides many of the issues that are inherent with gunite.

161

If the tile line were removed or left off of a pool that was built in a typical fashion, the gunite or marcite may develop the cracking and chipping at the frost line, as well a leave that unsightly ring around the pool. There are new methods of building where the interior pool finish is rolled right over the edge of the pool, so there is no need for tile in some cases.

---

160 The new tile is going on a freshly prepared surface for great adhesion
161 Karen, tile and coping specialist hangs over a pool to grout the tile lines while the pool is still full of water

Lifespan of Tile, Coping, Marcite and Pebble

162

Swimming pool tile, even when installed perfectly, can shift and fall off a pool in some cases within a year of being installed. Especially in freeze/thaw climates, even the most meticulous of installations cannot be guaranteed.

163

---

162 Clean tile and marcite in this just acid washed pool

The surface of the pool, whether marcite, pebble, or alternative finish should last 10-30+ years with proper care. Over time the water chemistry will affect the surface, and can cause etching or pitting in the surface. These are the lines or pock marks that show up in the pool.

These happen because when water conditions become aggressive, the water will pull minerals out of the surface of the pool, effectively eroding the surface. The surface may also become rough, either due to the etching or pitting, or in the reverse case, when water deposits minerals to the surface of the pool.

---

163 This pool step was cracked and etching, Karen is preparing the surface and adding a new layer of marcite.

Vinyl Liner Swimming Pool Renovation

A vinyl liner swimming pool renovation can include something as simple and straightforward as a liner replacement, or it can become more involved and include changing the coping and liner track style, repairing the bottom of the pool which is usually vermiculite {hard bottom} or sand, and in some cases concrete. Skimmers, return fittings, and lights are also the other areas where a vinyl liner pool can be renovated.

164

Vinyl Liner Replacements

Replace your vinyl liner and breathe new life into your pool. Prices vary depending on your exact pool conditions and specifications. Liners come in 20 Mil or 27/30 Mil thicknesses.

This is what is done during a typical liner replacement.

- ✓ Removal and disposal of old liner
- ✓ minor patching to hard-bottom
- ✓ installation of new liner
- ✓ replacement of gaskets and face plates
- ✓ cut in the liner
- ✓ fill the pool with water
- ✓ balance the water chemistry
- ✓ resume maintenance

---

164 Liner replacement before and after

Lifespan of Vinyl Liners

165

If a swimming pool liner is floating, it is often possible to drain the water from behind the liner and reset it. This is possible if the liner is newer (within 5 years of original installation). The typical vinyl liner will last up to 20 years, with the average being 10-12.

The longevity of the liner depends on the care of the liner, attention to water chemistry, and overall pool environment. Often a liner will fade and the pattern will become less visible

---

165 Hybrid swimming pool built by Legendary Escapes with In-Floor cleaning

due to the sun and chemical use. If a liner is torn or ripped, sometimes a patch can be used to lengthen the lifespan of the liner.

Once a liner gets older, it becomes less pliable and more brittle. In this instance, attempting to reset a floating liner could cause harm to the liner, and a full replacement would be recommended. It is also common to see liners start to pull away from the corners as they get older and more brittle. If the corner of a vinyl liner tears, patching will not usually hold, and the liner should be replaced.

pH Wrinkles in Vinyl Liners

Another issue which is often present in vinyl liners are small wrinkles covering either a small part, or sometimes the entire surface of the pool walls or floor. These are called pH wrinkles, and are caused when the water chemistry is not maintained in the proper balance. Once pH wrinkles form due to the liner absorbing water due to low pH, low alkalinity or stabilizer levels, or excessive use of bromine, there is no way to remove them, and the only option would be to replace the liner.

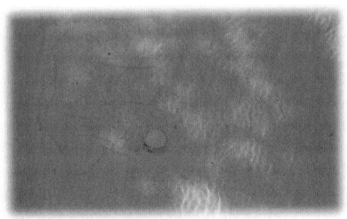

166

pH Wrinkles in a vinyl liner pool(above)

---

166 pH pool wrinkles

Homeowners often choose to perform vinyl liner pool renovations to address functional issues such as leaking or wrinkling, though many times it's purely aesthetic. If your family enjoys a pretty pool more than an older looking or dated pool, then it's always a great decision to make.

Vinyl Liner Coping/Track

167

When it is time for a renovation, the coping/liner track combination could be replaced by a new coping/liner track combo, but only if the liner and the concrete patio are both being replaced.

Other options include removing the existing coping and installing new coping in a variety of materials including stone, bluestone, pavers, or cantilever pool deck, and also installing a surface mount "coping" also known as "liner track" for the pool liner to track into.

Renovation Timing

---

[167] Vinyl liner coping track

Many homeowners ask what is the best time of year to perform a swimming pool renovation. The answer to this question has many variables. Anytime that it needs it is a great time to perform a swimming pool renovation project. You may want to take into consideration the climate, as most renovations are best done in favorable weather conditions, where it is warm enough that materials used are not so cold they are freezing and brittle, and not too hot that they are melting and sagging.

Late fall versus early spring is also a good time to think about a renovation. Once the summer is winding down and the pool has been enjoyed, it's much less stressful on the homeowner and the contractor if the renovation doesn't have to be rushed so the pool can be used. The weather conditions are often favorable, warm and dry, this time of year as well.

Early Spring Renovations & Ground Water Issues

Early spring when it is often the wettest is not the ideal time to perform a renovation on either a gunite or vinyl liner pool. Ground water pressure is a concern with a gunite pool. While it is essential that when draining a gunite pool {under the supervision or direction of a pool professional} that they hydrostatic relief valve in the bottom of the main drain functions to pop open and allow water in if the ground pressure is greater than the pressure holding the pool in place, it's also important that you choose the right conditions to even attempt this. Please don't think you are saving any time by draining your pool while you wait for quotes or a pool professional to come and evaluate your pool. It is never a good idea to empty a gunite swimming pool, unless you know exactly what you are doing.

Ground Water and Vinyl Liner Swimming Pools

The concern with wet conditions for a vinyl liner replacement are that once the liner comes out, if ground water starts pouring into the pool through cracks in the hard bottom aka Pre-Mix Vermiculite *Pool Floor*, or in between the steel walls it can cause issues with setting the liner properly and wrinkles. If ground water cannot be avoided there are several options, such a burying a pump under the pool, installing ancillary sump pumps near the pool to drain the water, or having a pump available during the installation to remove the water just long enough to get the new liner in and water on top of the liner to keep the ground water under control.

Floating Swimming Pool Liners

If you have a vinyl liner pool that experiences floating, it is a good idea to assess your yard and conditions.

It is possible that a floating liner is caused by a leak in the liner, a pin hole is enough to drain an entire swimming pool.

Other potential causes of a floating liner could be inadequate yard drainage, where the yard or patio slopes toward the pool rather than away from it. Gutters and downspouts on a home also protect the pool from the additional watershed that could occur. Broken underground sprinkler lines have also been found to cause water issues. If soil conditions are sand based, most water will drain away from under a pool relatively well. If the conditions are clay, or swampy with a high water table, some of the water remediation options may need to be explored.

168

There are invisible forces at work underneath your pool. These forces are known as hydrostatic pressure. This pressure is what forms cracks in the shell of your pool and bulges in your vinyl.

Vinyl liners actually have an advantage over fiberglass pools because there are several fairly simple fixes that can help with the hydrostatic pressure.

How Does This Happen?

Many people think that if your vinyl liner is floating then you have a groundwater problem. This isn't necessarily the case, sometimes the water is coming from the swimming pool itself.

How hydrostatic pressure affects a vinyl liner pool

As long as the water level in the pool is higher than the water level in the ground there will be enough water pressure inside the pool to keep the liner in place.

If your backyard doesn't have proper drainage and keep the water away from the pool, or in some cases, even move water toward the pool due to improper line placement, broken lines, or plugged drains, you may develop an issue.

Dealing with the elements and precipitation

---

168 Vinyl liner with ground water built up underneath the pool liner

If you have proper drainage, water from rain and melting snow should be diverted from your pool area and into an appropriate drain.

If the drainage is not present, then water may collect around your pool area, and add itself to the groundwater. If that happens, and the water swells above your pool's water level you will experience problems.

Water rising slightly higher than the water level in your pool, even as little as 1/8 of an inch could cause your liner to float or trap water[xviii].

How to Address Water Behind the Liner

The quick fix available is to run a pump between the liner and the pool wall. This removes the trapped water. Then you partially drain the pool to work out any of the wrinkles.

169

Another option is a well point. This provides a more permanent solution. In a well point, a 12 inch diameter pipe is inserted vertically into the ground. This provides a path for the water to well into. This is how it's done:

---

[169] Removing water behind the vinyl liner with the vac hose

- ✓ Drill a hole about 1 or 2 feet deeper than the pool's deep end. Make sure it's wide enough to accommodate the pipe circumference.
- ✓ Then add a 1 or 2 food layer of gravel in the bottom. Make sure this level is about three quarters of an inch.
- ✓ Install a 12 inch PVC pipe and backfill around it. If you have a case of extreme groundwater, add an 18 or 24 inch diameter pipe instead of a 12 inch pipe.
- ✓ An automatic submersible pump is then placed at the bottom.
- ✓ Set it up so it's triggered when water in the pipe reaches a certain level.
- ✓ You will need a horizontal discharge pipe near the top of the vertical installation. This channels the water offsite. If you put a lid on it, you're all set.

170

It's not always easy to determine the best location for the well point. Sometimes it's a guessing game; other times pipe placement is obvious. We hope you experience the latter. If you

---

[170] Sump drainage system

have a body of water in your yard like a creek or pond, place the well pipe in between the body of water and your pool.

A French drain is another option for aiding with groundwater. They are a drain that will allow surface water and subsurface water to enter a pipe and be redirected away from a pool.

First you have to dig a trench around the pool deeper than the level where you will want the final drain pipe. The depth of the trench depends on a couple factors: site conditions and how much water is present. Make sure the horizontal pipe is below the pool's water level, [171]and will be able to catch surface and subsurface water.

Landscape fabric is typically put into the bottom of the trench and covered with a layer of pervious gravel. This provides the water a path of least resistance (remember, water always chooses the path of least resistance). The fabric is needed to hold the gravel in place.

The drain pipe itself will have a series of holes. Make sure the holes are facing downward. This allows the water to seep up from the ground. It will then enter the trench and rise into the pipe. Make sure to channel the water into a solid drain pipe to carry it off correctly.

[171] French drain

For many of these groundwater suggestions, it is best to consult a professional to ensure the job is done correctly.

Bulging Pool Liners or Bubbles Under the Liner

Homeowners often mistake a bubble under the pool liner as air, when it is actually water.

You are more likely to notice a bulge or bubble in your vinyl liner after the winter season, especially if your pool level water was either lowered too much, or you developed a leak over the winter.

Professionals usually lower the water well below the skimmer and return lines when they close a pool. This method may work on steep sites that shed water easily but be weary if you have a flat property or the pool is at the lowest point of the surrounding yards.

Dropping the pool water too during winterization actually increases the chance of hydrostatic pressure. Make sure not to lower the pool water level lower than you actually need to, and avoid the use of a sump or cover pump on a plastic cover over the winter. Allowing the water to collect on the top of the cover is the best option.

Fiberglass Swimming Pool Renovation

There are not many options available for renovation of a fiberglass swimming pool. If you do ever drain a fiberglass pool, be very careful that you have the appropriate environment with the proper sump pumps and low ground water pressure so it doesn't become an issue.

If you develop a crack in a fiberglass pool, crack remediation is a technical process that will require an expert to repair.

The same is true for resurfacing a fiberglass pool. These specialties are in high demand, so be aware of that if you ever encounter this issue.

If your fiberglass pool gel coat develops a cloudy appearance, please contact your manufacturer for advice and instruction. We have had a customer in the past be advised to use a fine grit sand paper to remove the cloudy surface, though this was specific to his particular gel coat of his pool.

172

---

172 Fiberglass pool with hazy finish

ecoFINISH[xix]

ecoFINISH, a plastic powder coating process may be a good solution. Check with the manufacturer to see if there is a technician that offers this process in your area.

173

---

[173] ecoFinish thermoplastic application on a Legendary Escapes Sun Ledge

Hybrid Swimming Pool Renovation

We get many inquiries about renovating gunite and vinyl liner pools, and the ability to add sun ledges, and additional features to the pool. Sometimes this is an option, other times it would take major structural changes to accommodate the request.

In the case of a vinyl liner pool, the product Tru-Tile offered to a select number of builders via Latham Industries is one way of adding a ceramic tile line to a vinyl liner pool. This is also the system Ask the Pool Guy uses in building hybrid swimming pools that feature both vinyl liner and gunite components.

174

This cement walled, vinyl liner pool was converted into a hybrid swimming pool with a gunite sun shelf/step area, ceramic tile border, and vinyl liner. Prior to the renovation there was a ladder at each end for entry/exit, with the renovation there is a step/ledge area for easier entry and exit for older adults and children, and a place for grandkids to play in a shallow part of the pool. The plumbing was completely redone, as well as the coping and patio.

---

174 Brick wall vinyl liner swimming pool

Demolition started with removing the patio, the liner, and prepping the pool for shotcrete.

The new sun ledge and step are in, now to install the ceramic tile surround, and prep for liner installation.

Ceramic tile 6" and Quartzite Coping

The final product is a newly refinished pool for the entire family to enjoy.

175

Pool Equipment Troubleshooting Guide

Pump

Pump Suddenly Stops Working

Troubleshooting steps:

- ✓ Has your power gone out, or your breaker tripped?
- ✓ Has your equipment accidentally shut off? Check the power source.
- ✓ Is your water level low, causing your pump to lose prime? Fill the pool to your proper operational level.
- ✓ Have any of your valves been closed? Make sure all valves are open properly.
- ✓ Are all your baskets, in the skimmer and pump clean and clear of debris?
- ✓ Is your lid sealed on the pump?
- ✓ Is the pump full of water?
- ✓ Has your automation system experienced a power outage? If so, reset the time.
- ✓ Do you have an automatic timer? Make sure your dial is set to the right time and the on and off trippers are in the right time locations.
- ✓ Has something gotten stuck in your impeller? Carefully check this, making sure the power to the pump is off before you investigate.

If none of these help, call your pool service team for additional troubleshooting tips.

Pump Only Hums

- ✓ Is the breaker tripped? If so, reset the breaker. If it keeps tripping, check the electrical circuit. If the circuit appears fine, your pump may be indicating a serious issue and need to be replaced.

237

- ✓ A hum may indicate the thermal switch inside the pump motor is indicating something is wrong. The thermal switch's job is to turn the pump off to prevent further issues. A service call may be in order here.
- ✓ A hum may also indicate the motor can't spin. Taking apart the pump housing will allow you (or your service team) to check this out. Sometimes motors are stuck during a pool opening, and once they are loosened they operate properly. If they don't, a pump replacement may be indicated.

Pump runs but will not move water

- ✓ Pump may have lost its "Prime". With the pump motor off, prime your pump by removing the lid, and fill the pump with water until the pot is full. It may be helpful to force some water down your pipes as well to give the pump added water to draw when it turns back on.
- ✓ With your system off, check your skimmer to be sure it is free of debris or toys that will prevent the flow of water.
- ✓ Check your pump plugs to be sure they are air tight and you do not have any air leaks. Air in your pool pump will prevent it from priming and moving water properly.
- ✓ With your system off, move your multiport handle to recirculate to bypass your filter to determine if you have a filter blockage or malfunction. if you are able to get the pump to prime in this way, when water begins to run freely, turn pump off, place valve in filter position and turn pump back on.

Pump Is Loud

- ✓ Is the noise coming from the pump housing (the front of the pump) or is it coming from the

motor (the back of the pump)?

- ✓ A loud noise is usually the result of the bearings going out, in the motor.
- ✓ The loud noise could also be caused by the impeller being out of place, grinding, or caught with debris. Call your pool service team for help.
- ✓ Is the pump sucking air? Make sure the level of the pool water is at the standard operating water level (at least half way up the skimmer).
- ✓ Make sure that the pump and skimmer baskets are clean.
- ✓ Make sure all of the valves are fully open.
- ✓ Make sure that the lid O-ring is in place and that the lid is properly sealed.
- ✓ If everything seems okay, *cavitation* may be occurring-where the pump is struggling to circulate more water than is available to it. There can be a number of causes for cavitation, and your pool service team can help troubleshoot this.

The Breaker Keeps Tripping

- ✓ If it keeps tripping, check the electrical circuit. If the circuit appears fine, your pump may be indicating a serious issue and need to be replaced.

Filter

Frequent Need for Filter Cleaning/Backwashing

- ✓ Make sure your water chemistry is on target.
- ✓ If pH, Alkalinity, or Hardness levels are high, scale may develop in the plumbing, restricting flow, causing filtration issues.
- ✓ Determine the time since your last sand change, DE filter clean, or cartridge replacement. It might be time.
- ✓ Is your chlorine level low, or do you have algae present in your pool?
- ✓ Did you just add stabilizer? This will cause an increase in your filter pressure.
- ✓ Did you just add a chemical that has an increase in filter pressure as a byproduct?
- ✓ Are you backwashing and rinsing long enough when you are performing filter maintenance? Only clean your filter when your pressure gauge shows a pressure increase of 5-7psi above your standard operating pressure.

Sand filter:

- ✓ Has the correct sand been used? "Playground" sand will not work. You need to purchase the proper silica sand from your local pool professionals, and install it in the proper amounts.
- ✓ Is the sand too old? It might have debris impeding the flow of water, or channeling and need a sand or filter media change.

DE filter:

- ✓ Are you using the correct amount of DE powder?
- ✓ Too much DE powder will not sit properly on the DE grids, which will reduce the effectiveness of the DE powder, causing a shorter filter run between cleanings.
- ✓ Has your DE filter had a thorough filter cleaning? It might be time to really service your filter.

✓ Are your DE grids in good condition, or old, worn or torn. These can only be checked during a DE filter clean, so consider doing that next.

Cartridge filter:

✓ When is the last time your filter elements have been cleaned?
✓ Is it time to replace them?
✓ Have you added a product to your pool to floc or coagulate metals? This is a common cause of impeding the function of a cartridge filter.
✓ Are your cartridge filter pleats torn or frayed? Time to replace.
✓ Are your cartridge filter bases or any parts torn or damaged? Time to replace.

Sand Is On The Floor Of The Pool

(For those of you with a sand filter only)

✓ A lateral, which is at the bottom of your sand filter, has either cracked or is broken, allowing sand to pass through the filter, enter the return (plumbing) lines, and enter the pool, via the return jets. Either way, all the sand has to be removed. Then, each lateral must be removed and inspected in order to determine which lateral(s) are cracked or broken. Once found and replaced, the sand has to be put back into the filter. If it has been a few years since your last sand change it is time to do a sand change as well. Sand changes should be done every 3-5 years or as problems present with your filter.
✓ When sand was last added, was it the correct amount? Overfilled filters can force sand through into the pool.
✓ Is your pump running at the correct speed or strength? Especially with new variable speed pumps it is possible to overstress a filter, especially if it is not sized for additional water flow. Run the pump at a slower speed to see if it prevents the issue.
✓ You may not be backwashing or rinsing long enough.

✓ If your sand is fine like silt, it may be debris coming back through your filter system.
✓ When replacing the sand, be careful. The weight of the sand could crack or break your laterals, and cause the issue without you knowing the damage occurred.
✓ If you do add sand to the filter yourself, add water to the filter to just cover the laterals, and then slowly add sand, being careful not to get any into the center filter tube.

DE Powder Is On The Floor Of The Pool

(For those of you with a DE filter only).

✓ Are your DE Grids torn or frayed?
✓ Have you added too much DE to your filter?
✓ Is your manifold within the DE tank damaged?
✓ Did you spill last time you added DE to the pool?

If any of the above are the case, DE filter service is in order.

Heater

Heater Will Not Heat

Check these areas first:

- ✓ Is the supply (natural gas, propane, or electricity) on? If not, turn it on.
- ✓ Is the pilot light lit? If not, light the pilot light. This is only for those heaters that require a manual ignition of the pilot light.
- ✓ Are the skimmer and pump baskets clean? If not, clean the skimmer and pump baskets. Full baskets will restrict water circulation. The pressure switch in the heater requires sufficient circulation for the heater to heat.
- ✓ Is the filter dirty? If so, clean (backwash a sand or DE filter, rinse Cartridge filter cartridges. A clogged filter will also restrict water circulation. Again, the pressure switch in the heater requires sufficient circulation for the heater to heat.
- ✓ Is the water level sufficient? If not, fill the pool to the standard operating water level, which is at least half way up your skimmer.
- ✓ Is anything impeding the flow of water in your plumbing? Sometimes small pool toys or acorns can find their way into the pipes.
- ✓ Are the valves open? If not, open all the valves.

If you check all of these and the heater still won't heat, please call for additional troubleshooting from your pool service team.

176

[177]A heater is kept in good running order by using it. If the heater is not used, rust will appear, spider webs and nests may be found, and mechanical parts may wear.

If water chemistry is out of balance, the heat exchanger could be corroded to the point of premature failure. This is an expensive replacement and another good reason to monitor your water chemistry.

Water Loss - Leaks and

---

[176] Mark servicing this swimming pool heater
[177] Heater full of nests and debris from rodents and insects

Evaporation

Pool Evaporation Rates

Every pool will experience water loss at some point. Normal water loss is caused by evaporation and splash out. It's normal for swimming pools to lose a quarter inch (1/4") or so of water each day. Wind, sunlight, and humidity can affect this loss. In a swimming pool with a waterfall or spillover spa this may increase even more.

The amount of evaporation will depend on your geographic and environmental factors. If you notice significant water loss, you will want to perform a bucket test to determine if it is a leak or evaporation. If you are constantly needing to fill your pool (more than 1/4" per day) you are more likely to have a leak.

If you don't think wind is the problem, sunlight and humidity can also cause water evaporation/water loss. Humidity is the amount of moisture in the air. When the air is 'humid' water molecules stay in place. If you live in humid areas, your pool's water molecules will stay put in the pool. If you are in a dry, arid area, water molecules will evaporate at a much higher rate. Sunlight will also speed up the process of evaporation.

Products such as solar covers or liquid solar blankets can form a layer of protection over your pool and reduce the effects of evaporation in your pool.

Leaks

Leaks at your Equipment

If you have a leak at your equipment, determine where the leak is coming from.

If it appears to be coming from a threaded plug, turn the equipment off and either use a water based lubricant, or Teflon tape on the threads and attempt to resecure the plug.

[178]If your leak is at connectors or fittings, you may need to tighten the fitting.

Pool Putty or Silicone will sometimes stop a slow leak. Anything more than a trickle that remains may need to be addressed and fittings or plumbing replaced.

Leaks in your Pool or Plumbing

Pool Leak Detection

Water loss is normal from evaporation, at the rate of .25" or less per day, unless you are in the hottest part of summer, at which time you may experience more loss from evaporation. Your rate may vary depending on the surface area of your pool, temperature of your air and water during the day and at night, the humidity and the wind.

Water loss will also be experienced when you have swimmers, from normal use and splashing that may occur.

You will also lose water from running a waterfall or spa, and this amount of loss will increase during hot, or windy weather when the spray may be carried away by the wind.

Using a product such as Natural Chemistry's Cover Free will help prevent water loss by evaporation. You can also use plastic solar covers for this purpose (they are just cumbersome and harder to handle.)

If you think you are losing water:

---

[178] Pool putty on a pipe repair

- ✓ Fill the pool to your normal operating level and mark the level on your skimmer with a sharpie marker.
- ✓ Run the system as normal and recheck the level in 24 hours, note the amount of water loss.
- ✓ Next, turn off your system and determine if the pool continues leaking, and how much in a 24 hour period.

Bucket Test for Water Loss

[179]To compare your water loss with that of normal evaporation, you can perform the bucket test.

To perform a bucket test:

- ✓ Take a 5-gallon bucket and make a mark with a permanent marker at about the halfway point.
- ✓ Fill the bucket with (pool water so it's the same temperature) water up to that point, and set the bucket right beside your swimming pool or on your swimming pool step.
- ✓ Simultaneously, use a sharpie marker or duct tape to mark the water level on your pool tile.
- ✓ In that way, you can determine how much water has evaporated from the bucket and from the pool.
- ✓ **If you are running your heater continually during this process, and your air temperature is causing steam to billow off your pool this will not be an accurate way to measure your evaporation.
- ✓ Leave the bucket and pool running for 24 hours, and compare the amount of water loss in each. If they lost at the same rate, congratulations, no leak. If the pool lost more than the bucket, you have more troubleshooting to do.

---

[179] Bucket test for evaporation vs. swimming pool leak

- ✓ To determine if the leak is in your pool structure, or in your pool plumbing, repeat the test with your swimming pool OFF.

A few fun facts:

- ✓ We have seen municipal reports suggesting a typical loss of loss of 200-300 gallons per week for a medium-sized pool — which is between 2%-5% of typical pool volumes in southern states. Northern pools tend to be on the larger side with volumes from 15,000-30,000+ gallons.
- ✓ You will lose more water in the spring and fall than in the middle of summer. When water temperatures warm up during the day and cool significantly at night just watch the steam rising. (I often visualize this as $$ signs floating right out of the pool.)
- ✓ Liquid Solar Blankets and plastic solar blankets are a great way to prevent a significant amount of evaporation.
- ✓ [180]A call to your local pool professional to troubleshoot your questions may help give you an idea what is normal for your area.
- ✓ Leak detection experts can use equipment to locate and find leaks through the use of underwater microphones and other technical equipment.

---

[180] Getting ready for a deep end leak detection dive

Underwater light goes out

- ✓ Check switch, circuit breaker or check the GFCI. (your outlets are often on the same circuit as your pool light, so check your outlet and reset if available.
- ✓ Check and possibly replace your light bulb, or in some cases your entire light fixture.

181

In-Floor Cleaning Heads are Stuck

- ✓ Make sure the filter is functioning properly. Backwash if needed.
- ✓ Check the valve to make sure it has proper water flow and movement.
- ✓ Remove individual cleaning heads and check for stuck pebbles or debris.

182

---

181 Corroded light ring and major cord issues with this in pool light. Time for replacement!

FAQ

Salt Water Pools and Chlorine Generating Systems

How Saltwater Pools Work

By adding a chlorine generator to your pool's plumbing system, the generator works with salt added to the water to produce the active chlorine required to keep your pool water clean, so you don't need to continually add chlorine and other chemicals. You don't have to specifically do anything prior to the installation of a salt system, though keeping your water in balance is always recommended.

[183]The conversion will start by installing the chlorine generator along side of your other pool equipment.

It's installed in your pool's water return lines (after the filter and heater) by cutting into the return lines and installing PVC piping to run water through the chlorine generator then back into the return line. The generator needs a power source, so it will be wired into the pool pump circuit, so that the generator turns on and off at the same times as the pool pump.

Then you'll need to add salt to your pool. The amount of salt your pool requires depends on the size of your pool. Estimate 50 pounds of salt per 1,200 gallons of capacity. Yes, that may sound (and look) like a lot of salt. It's close to adding only one

---

[182] InFloor Cleaning Heads
[183] Hybrid Swimming Pool built by Legendary Escapes Pools

teaspoon of salt to one gallon of water. Many people will not even be able to taste the salt.

Once installed, turning on the pump circulates the salt water through the system, including the chlorine generator. Magic? No, chemistry.

Through an electrolysis process, the salt molecules (sodium chloride) are separated into sodium and chlorine.

Concurrently, a hydrogen atom is freed from the water molecules.

Know that the hydrogen and chloride atoms combine to form sodium hypochlorite (chlorine) that actually purifies the water in your pool. After sanitizing your pool water, the chlorine chemically recombines with sodium, turns back into salt, and the process begins all over again.

Benefits:

- ✓ Because the cell generates chlorine, the homeowner doesn't need to buy, store or handle chlorine.
- ✓ When shocking is needed, units have a super-chlorinate function that can be triggered.
- ✓ Chlorine is produced when the system is running, so there is a continual dispersing of chlorine.

Drawbacks:

- ✓ Chlorine is produced when the system is running. If the system is off, chlorine is not being made.

Since salt water conducts electricity, a zinc anode must be added to prevent electrolysis.

Metals:

Metals in a salt water pool (handrails, metal parts of equipment) will you essentially create a battery. A small current will flow between metals. Though it is safe to swim in

[184]Some amount of current flows between the metals. Don't worry: the levels of electricity present are perfectly safe to swim in and will be undetected by swimmers.

Metals in your pool will be affected. Electrons that make up the current are supplied by metals in the pool, starting with the weakest metal, which is forced to give up bits of itself in the form of metal ions. This process is galvanic corrosion and will cause plaster discoloration and metal erosion.

Heater cores are especially affected by this, as the copper heater core is the weakest.

An electrical charge through water also pulls whatever is in water out of solution, so electrolysis will cause calcium to come out of solution and cause scaling on pool surfaces.

[185]Zinc Anode

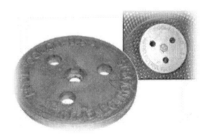

A zinc anode is a crucial part of any salt pool. The best option is one that gets plumbed into your equipment–this type of anode will best protect your pool and equipment from the negative effects of electrolysis.

Another option, less expensive but less effective, is a disc-shaped zinc anode that sits in your skimmer basket.

---

[184] Zinc Anode for electrolysis prevention
[185] Basket weight zinc anode

Zinc anodes are also called sacrificial anodes, because they corrode instead of the other metals in your pool. Zinc is a weak metal, so the anode sacrifices itself to galvanic corrosion so the [186]other metals in your pool and equipment don't have to. It also helps to prevent calcium scaling. This is an absolute must for a salt water pool!

How salty is a salt water pool?

The salt level for a safe, chlorinated pool is about 2,500 to 4,000 PPM (parts per million). Most people can't taste salt until the PPM is around 5,000. So for most people, it's not even noticeable. It freaks a lot of people out to dump salt directly into their pools, especially in the quantity that is necessary. But it's important to remember how many gallons are in your pool. With the huge quantity of water in a swimming pool, the ratio of salt to water is about a teaspoon per gallon. If you're worried about how salty your pool might taste, you can test it by simply putting a teaspoon of salt into a gallon of water.

 You only need to add salt to your pool or spa if your control box indicates your levels are low or, obviously, you have completely (or significantly) drained your pool.

Here is how to figure out how much salt you would need after just filling it with fresh water.

If you don't already know, estimate how many gallons your pool holds.

The formula (using feet) is:

Average Depth x Length x Width x 7.5 = Gallons

---

[186] Basket zinc anode weight with corrosion

The average depth = (depth at shallow end + depth at deep end) divided by 2

Example:

The pool is 50' long and 20' wide. The shallow end is 3' and the deep end is 9'.

Average depth = (3' + 9') / 2 = 6'

6' x 50' x 20' x 7.5 = 45,000 gallons.

If this is a new pool, you will need 50 lbs salt for every 2,000 gallons to get about 4,000 ppm, a good starting point. So for this example, you would need 1,125 lbs of salt

For existing pools, the previous usage of chlorine bleach or tablets will have already created a level of salt in the water. Have the water tested and then add the appropriate amount to establish 4,000 ppm.

Example:

The measurement for this same pool is 3,000 ppm.

So you need to add 1,000 ppm or ¼ of the example above = about 280 lbs

Once your salt level is established, there is no need to add salt unless the pool is drained or loses a significant amount of water. The most common ways you lose salt is through leaks, rainwater overflow, filter backwash, fun-time splashing, and what leaves on everyone's swimsuit. Evaporation does not lose salt, it just increases the concentration. Add water to reduce the salt concentration back to 4000 ppm. Most chlorine generator units have low salt indicators and the digital type even give you the proper amount of salt needed to return to 4000 ppm.

How do I add the salt?

Pour it in. Agitation, sweeping, or brushing will help the salt dissolve faster. It will happen even faster if you turn on the pump, open the bottom drain, and add the salt over the drain. Running the pump for about 24 hours will dissolve it evenly throughout the pool. Granular salt will dissolve 60 – 70% before even hitting bottom. The remaining salt can simply be brushed into the drain. Other forms of salt, take longer to dissolve but the same actions will make apply.

pH/Total Alkalinity in Salt Water Pools

The pH and Alkalinity need to be constantly monitored to make sure they stay in optimal operating levels for the pool. Muriatic Acid or pH reducer needs to be added most often since the generator is making liquid chlorine with a pH of about 13%, by the time it affects the pool it's about 8.5%, which is above the optimal level of 7.4 in a pool. This can be added by hand, or there is a dispenser unit available that will do it automatically as well.

Maintenance

This is another bonus of Chlorine Generators: they require almost no maintenance. We recommend the generator cell be removed and cleaned on a yearly basis. The best time to do this is when you open your pool. Simply remove the cell from the pool plumbing and run a plastic brush through it. If you notice calcium deposits, a mild solution of muriatic acid and water will clean it up. You can also use the Lo-Chlor Green Cell Plus. The actual power supply unit requires no regular maintenance.

FAQ's

What type of salt do I add?

We definitely recommend avoiding rock salt because it contains too many impurities. The best salts to use include: food grade salt, water softener pellets, solar salt flakes, water conditioner salt, or brine blocks. Be sure to add salt with no iodine and also that it is as pure as possible.

How/where do I add the salt?

The key factor in adding salt to your pool water is to brush the salt around until it is completely dissolved- you don't want any remaining salt particles to be settled on your pool floor. This can be accelerated by turning on your pump, opening the bottom drain, and adding the salt over the drain. This is much easier than walking around the perimeter while adding the salt. We recommend you run the pump for around 24 hours so the salt can be spread evenly throughout the pool. If you're using granular salt, almost 70% of it will dissolve before hitting the bottom. The remaining salt can simply be brushed into the drain. If you're using any other form of salt, it will take longer to dissolve but the same process will do the trick.

How much salt do I add?

We recommend adding enough for 4,000 PPM as a starting point. If you are starting off with a higher salt level in your pool, only add the amount needed to reach 4,000 PPM. For existing pools, the previous use of chlorine will have already created a level of salt in the water. Have the water tested first to see the salt level, then simply add the appropriate amount of salt. You can test the salt level using salt test strips, or contact Ask the Pool Guy and we can handle it for you!

What if I accidentally add to much salt?

[187]Don't worry, over salting will not harm your chlorine generator. However, it will most likely lead to salty tasting water. For some people, this is not undesirable and they might enjoy it. For others, it can create discomfort. If you added a

great amount of extra salt (over 6,000 PPM), you might begin to see corrosion damage to metallic equipment. To reduce the salt level, dilution is the key. Drain some of your over-salted water and replenish it with fresh water until you reach the ideal 4,000 PPM.

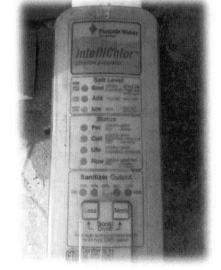

How often do I add salt?

After your initial large dosage of salt, you will need to add

---

[187] IntelliChlor salt generating cell

more when your salt system calls for more.

The most common ways salt is lost is through leaks, rainwater overflow, filter backwashing, and too much splashing. Normal water evaporation does not lose salt, in fact, it can increase the salt concentration. Most chlorine generators have low salt indicators making it easy for you to tell when you may need to add some.

Does this eliminate the need to add chemicals?

NO. Chlorine generators do just one thing, generate chlorine. Because this chlorine is very pure, fewer chemicals are needed to keep the water balanced. So having a chlorine generator does not eliminate the need to use chemicals in your pool but it can lessen it significantly. It is also important to check the total alkalinity and calcium hardness of your pool monthly. In some situations, you might need to shock the pool due to rainstorms, accidents, or many swimmers. Shocking your pool will not affect your chlorine generator.

Will I have to use more energy?

If your chlorine generator is properly sized to your pool, you will not need extended pump time. This means you will likely use the same amount of energy your pool is already using. Most chlorine generators have multiple configuration set-ups so that you can generate sufficient amounts of chlorine during your current pump circulation time.

How long will the Chlorine Generator last?

Residential cells are rated for about 10,000 hours of operation. This usually means around 3-5 years. It all depends on the size of your pool and the sanitizer demands of your pool. Water chemistry balance is key in ensuring a maximum cell life. The harder you use and run the cell, the shorter the lifespan. Annual inspection and cleaning is a great way to extend the life of your chlorine generator.

What is a Zinc Anode?

[188]A zinc anode is an important part of your chlorine generating system. It is protects the metal components of your swimming pool from corrosion. The zinc anode will be the first thing to corrode, saving the other parts of your pool from corrosion. We are happy to quote a salt system if you might want to convert your pool to a salt/chlorine generating pool. If you have a salt pool already – double check to make sure you have a zinc anode. They are often overlooked, and are a critical part of your system!

Do I need a Zinc Anode on a Salt Water Pool?

Yes, you ABSOLUTELY MUST have a zinc anode on a salt water pool! One option for a zinc anode is a small round disc that is secured in your skimmer basket – it's a small, yet important part of the system.

The other way to include a zinc anode in a system is to plumb it in with the plumbing. Slightly more work to install, but this way you are sure not to lose it.

For those of you that have a salt pool. Here is the reason why you need a zinc anode. It becomes the sacrifice for trade electrical charges in the water. Without it trace electrical attacks metal parts of the pool.

---

[188] Zinc Anode for plumbing into a pool system

Taking Care of Your Saltwater Pool

Maintaining chlorine generating systems is simple. Modern systems test for salt levels and have indicator lights to let you know if salt levels need to be adjusted. Many chlorine generating systems are self-cleaning as well, using a built-in polarity reversal function to clean themselves. If your system doesn't have a self-cleaning function, and even if it does, your cell will need to have a muriatic acid wash every season or two to clean any corrosion or build up off of the internal components.

If you don't feel you are getting accurate readings with your salt system itself (which sometimes happens when components need to be replaced) you can test the salt level in your water periodically, using salt test strips available at pool supply stores.

Recommended Product:

IntelliChlor Salt Chlorine Generator

189

The IntelliChlor Salt Chlorinator uses salt to produce all the chlorine a pool needs, safely, effectively, and automatically. It has the same sanitation performance as manually adding chlorine, without the drawbacks. No need for customers to buy, transport, store, and dump in chlorine compounds. Result: fewer resources are used in the production, packaging, and transportation of these chemical compounds.

---

189 IntelliChlor Salt Chlorinator, all systems GO!

Calculating Water Volume

Do you know how many gallons of water are in your pool?

Anytime you take in a water sample, or have a discussion about adding chemicals to your pool, and the amount of filtration your pool needs it is good to know the approximate water volume of your pool.

To assist in calculating the approximate gallons of water in your pool, here are pool industry-endorsed formulas based on the shape of your pool:

For a rectangle, multiply your length (in feet) times the width (in feet) times average depth (in feet) times 7.5.

For a round/oval, multiply your length (in feet) times the width (in feet) times average depth (in feet) times 5.9.

To determine average depth add the shallow end depth plus the deep end depth and divide by 2.

Example: (3' + 8' = 11'/2= 5.5'average depth)

Rectangle / Roman-End / Grecian / Square

Length x Width x Average depth x **7.5**

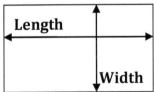

Round

Depth x Diameter x Diameter x **5.9**

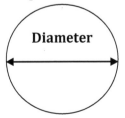

Oval

Longest Length x Longest Width x Average Depth x **5.9**

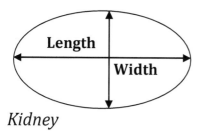

Kidney

Longest Length x Longest Width x Average Depth x **5.9**

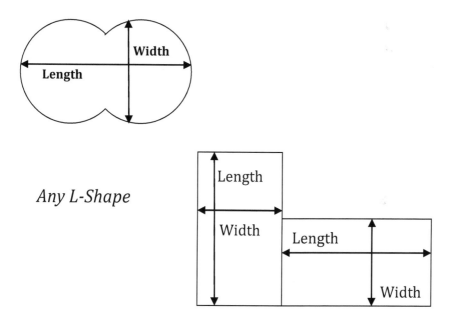

Any L-Shape

Break the "L" into two separate rectangles (or squares). Then, use the formula for a rectangle (or square) for each section. Finally, add the two sections together.

Length x Width x Average Depth x 7.5 + Length x Width x Average Depth x 7.5

Free Form Or Irregular Shapes

Consult with the pool professional that built your pool, as they may have the dig diagrams or spec sheets on file that list the total gallons.

If you can't get the volume this way, use the circular shape formula, or that for the kidney can do your best to compute from that. It will get you pretty close.

When you are having your water tested on a regular basis, they will usually ask you what your water volume is. You also need to know this so you can adjust your chemicals as needed. There are some simple formulas to figure out water volume.

If your pool is freeform, you will be somewhere in the middle of the two formulas. Does your pool resemble a rectangle more, or an oval more? Once you choose a formula, you may have to adjust a bit if your pool has smaller areas or larger curves outside the length and width that you used.

Of course the way to know the exact volume of water your pool takes is to have it filled with a water truck which can only fit so many gallons onto their truck, or if you have metered water, fill the pool and you'll see what you have been charged for.

Example Pool Water Volume Calculation

190

The pool pictured above is approximately 18×36 freeform with a 3.5' shallow end, and 7' deep end. To figure the water volume on this pool the Pool Guy would use the formula for a rectangle, and shorten the length and width a bit to compensate for the curves. The water volume of the pool can be estimated at 22,000-25,000 gallons, and the attached spillover spa at 300 gallons.

---

190 Vinyl liner pool with raised spillover spa and water feature built by Legendary Escapes

How Much Water Should be in My pool?

Your pool needs the right amount of water for several reasons. The structure of your pool whether fiberglass, gunite or vinyl needs an optimal amount of water to prevent any damage, shifts in the pool, floating of liners, or pool pop outs. We know some manufacturers or installers say a gunite or fiberglass pool will never pop out of the ground, however there is a term for it, and you can find plenty of photos online, so it can happen. It shouldn't though, especially if you keep your pool as full as possible at all times (spring, summer, fall and WINTER).

The equipment of your pool needs enough water flowing to run all the components properly. The pool will draw water from the main drain, and from the skimmer simultaneously. It is important to keep an eye on objects that may obstruct your main drain and skimmer, and to watch that the water level in the skimmer opening remains high enough to provide enough water flow through your pump and into your filter and additional equipment.

Skimmer Water Level

The correct operating level for your water at the skimmer(s) will vary depending on your pool set up.

As a general rule, you need enough water in the pool so when water is drawn through the skimmer(s) you don't create a whirlpool or suck air into the pipe.

Sometimes a pool looks full, but when the pump starts pulling water through the skimmer(s), it is pulling so fast that the skimmer can't refill fast enough. If you get any hissing, gurgling, or sucking noises from your skimmer, chances are something is obstructing the water flow or you don't have enough water in the skimmer.

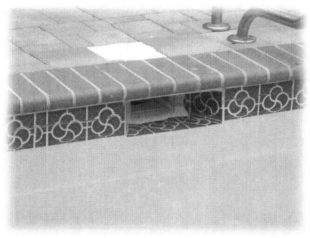

191

Gunite Pool and Skimmer Baskets with 2 Parts

In gunite pools with the two part skimmer basket, the top of the basket often gets stuck in an awkward angle, and also can prevent proper water flow. We have seen this cause loss of prime in a pump on more than one occasion.

The water level should also be, just low enough, that debris such as floating leaves can pass under the upper level of the skimmer(s) so that it can be caught in the skimmer basket, which is normally 3/4 full. If you are not sure of the proper level for your pool, you can always call your pool service team for guidance.

If you valves are set up to give you the option, you should be able to isolate the main drain and skimmer drain. These are the two valves typically located in front of your pump that bring water from the pool into your equipment system.

This is especially helpful in the spring when you are performing your pool opening, and you can isolate the main drain from the skimmer. If your skimmer ever falls too low to operate properly, you can temporarily close the valve to draw water only from the main drain to keep your water flow

---

[191] Gunite swimming pool with water 1/2 to 3/4 up the skimmer

functional for your pump. Just remember to reopen the skimmer valve when you refill the pool or you'll wonder why there is so much surface debris on top of your pool water.

Zip Tie Tip

Remember, you can use a zip tie as the Pool Girl did to indicate which line is your skimmer so you don't have to play a guessing game when you get out to your equipment each time.

Zip tie tip is also a tongue twister. Repeat that 3x fast.

Valves

Parallel = Open and Perpendicular = Closed

With typical valves, parallel with the pipe means open, and perpendicular means closed.

192

Three Way or Black Handled Valves that indicate OFF

In some valves with three way options, or the black handles you will note that one part of the handle says off. That means whichever pipe it is pointing to is in the closed position.

Many black handled valves also accommodate the automation function of automatic turning of valves for swimming pools with automation systems.

193

Pool/Spa Combination System

If you have a pool and spa combination, you will have a skimmer and main drain for your pool and typically a main drain for your spa. You will then have a system of return lines and waterfall/water feature lines that go back to the pool and separate lines that will go to a spa, and spa overflow waterfall if you have a spillover spa option.

194

Water In = Water Out

The important thing to note with your pool system as well is that if you have water coming into your pump, you must have valves open for water to return to the pool. It is important that you do not have conflicting valves, or the possibility of accidentally closing everything after your pump - this can cause huge issues. Your pump pushes a high volume of water at a high pressure. If the lines are not open to return to the pool,

---

194 Pool with raised spillover spa

something has to give and we have seen filter lids burst off at very high pressure, which is a dangerous situation.

Monitor your pool water level daily. Add water if it gets too low. If you notice that you are losing more than 1/4" of water a day, you may have a leak or other issue causing excessive water loss. Some leak detection and trouble-shooting will be in order.

Remember, some water will evaporate, this is normal.

Some water will splash out during use of the pool.

If you have backwashed your pool, vacuumed on waste, or done a rinse cycle, you will have wasted some water from the pool. When you are performing this type of maintenance is a great time to add water to your pool.

Should I ever drain all of the water in my pool?

[195]**NO!**

It doesn't matter which type of pool you have, draining your pool is a really bad idea, unless you have a plan and specific reasons for draining your pool, and you understand the risks that you are taking.

This pool, on the left, is having its liner replaced, which is a pretty good reason for a professional to empty your pool. If you drain your vinyl liner pool on your own for cleaning, you may have just created the need for an actual liner replacement, as your liner will not move back into position or become wrinkle free once you have drained it.

---

[195] Empty vinyl liner pool during a liner replacement

IMPORTANT: You should not drain a pool unless you have a very specific reason to do so, and/or you are doing it with the assistance of a pool professional.

Fiberglass Pools

A fiberglass pool with no water in it is like a giant bathtub, and if the water pressure in the ground is more than the force keeping the pool in the ground, you can have what is known as a "pop out". This is very expensive problem to have to address.

196

Gunite Pools

The same is true for a gunite pool. The gunite pools are usually equipped with a hydrostatic valve, it job is to pop open if the ground water pressure is more than the water in the pool. Providing this valve is working properly, you should be fine,

---

196 Fiberglass pool pop out, yes it does happen

but you really have no way of knowing unless it happens to engage. Sometime, we have also seen this valve work in reverse - after it popped open to allow the ground water pressure to be relieved, it also trapped a small stone in the valve and got stuck open, which proceeded to empty the gunite pool.

197

Draining During and Acid Wash

If you choose to perform an acid wash on a gunite pool, it is best to do the entire process in one day, and get water back in as soon as possible. Avoid performing the acid wash and draining of the pool if you have a high water table, or if you have any doubt that your hydrostatic relief valve will work.

---

[197] Gunite pool pop out, yes it can happen

[198]When our service team is doing a remarcite or repebble job, our crews will also often drill holes in the bottom of the gunite pool to allow any ground water to come through the holes while work is being performed. Rather little holes that are easy to fill, than big cracks that are not. Sometimes drilling these holes results in geysers spurting through the pool floor - indicating that indeed there is a water table and pressure present.

On the right, a gunite pool getting an acid wash. The gentleman in the corner, closest to the acid, is wearing a face mask for safety.

Vinyl Liner Pool Fixes

A vinyl liner pool is the least expensive (at several thousand dollars versus tens of thousands) to fix if you "accidentally drain the pool" or if you have problems.

The liner depends on water, to keep it set properly in the bottom of the pool. If you drain a liner pool, the liner can shift

---

[198] Drain and Clean Acid wash with Rick, Mark and Dave

and cause wrinkles or trap bubbles under the liner. Is this a major problem? Not really, the pool should still be able to function and hold water, but it may not be pretty or aesthetically pleasing.

199

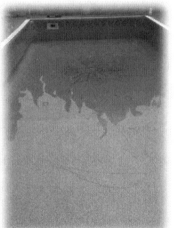

[200]If you have continuous water problems under the liner, you may need to address the drainage or add a sump pump system to help handle the ground water. In a worst case scenario, if you need to replace a liner you are talking a few thousand of dollars. A

---

[199] This vinyl liner pool was emptied by the homeowner to clean it. Once it was empty they figured out why this was a terrible idea.
[200]The result of resetting the liner, the wrinkles are here to stay until the liner is replaced.

fiberglass or gunite pool would take tens of thousands.

Swimming Pool Service Companies

The best time to call your pool company is when you have an issue, or when you are planning service for the future. Sometimes if it is the busiest part of opening season, you may be better off waiting until after the rush if you have a service request that is not time sensitive.

The best time to get a quote for service or renovation is anytime during the year. Most pool companies start planning in the fall for the spring projects, so if you are looking to swim early in the season, you want to reserve your spot during the previous season. Keep in mind that many things can affect spring construction, including the weather, ground conditions, frost laws, and the swimming pool builder's schedule.

Once you have a relationship with a pool company and they have become your service provider, you can call in anytime and usually be put on the top of the list, as each swimming pool company typically maintains a list of customers, and has services that they specialize in. Some companies are more technically savvy than others, so the level of your service will depend on the trade practices of the company you call.

If you become a "regular" or as we call them at Ask the Pool Guy, one of our "VIP Owners," these are people and pools we know well. If a service request comes in from one of these customers, we already have an idea how to handle the issue and what to expect on site, and it is easy to prioritize these to the top of our list.

Photos for Service Efficiency

Our service team takes photos at each pool we visit so we can maintain a database of pools and equipment. This helps us on future service call visits, as well as troubleshooting over the phone. We also ask for new callers to send in photos of their

275

pool and equipment so we can become familiar with the pool and system before we come out for a service call. We are also able to quote most issues by looking over the photos - and confirm on a service visit.

We also ask for email addresses. This isn't to send unwanted messages, but to send over quotes and information as it pertains to the pool and services we can provide. If you company asks for your email address, we have a hunch it will be for a similar reason.

If a service company is unfamiliar with a pool, they need to send someone out who can diagnose what is going on with a pool and how to best handle it on the spot, in many cases. This service person's time is very valuable, especially in peak pool season. There's a balance between visiting pools to give quotes (meaning money later, maybe) and sending a qualified service tech out to do an installation that results in a billable visit. There's a balance of both, however, the best time to get quotes is when the phones are slower.

201

---

[201] Taking photos during pool service

For example: There are 50,000 plus pools in Michigan's five county area (Oakland, Washtenaw, Wayne, Macomb and Livingston.) The average service company in the area can service about 500 customers very effectively. If you use Google or even word of mouth, and ask around, there are a handful of companies that get recommended. There's certainly room for more service companies in the area, though for now, let's deal with what we've got to work with (more about the new service business plan being launched by our company later).

If you can imagine, the minute the sun starts shining in May, all 50,000 pools are opened (in a window of about 30-45 days). This is when you find the issues, service calls, and troubleshooting appointments. That's trying to funnel a whole lot of people through a very narrow service window. (Who was calling in March and April - when were available?! Once the danger of frozen water pipes is over, a pool can be opened. You can always put a safety cover back on. In warm winter/spring years this is a very good thing to get a jump on algae growth.)

So what can you do to encourage quick service and turnaround of your request?

Create a relationship

Once you find a good service company, stick with them and let them get to know you and your pool. That means when you call we can diagnose over the phone and predict what your needs might be. This means less time for both of us because we'll have the right things on the truck. Customer loyalty also means that we'll be loyal to you, and fixing your issue quickly, if you've been loyal to us. If you are always seeking the lowest price and jumping from company to company, it costs both of us more time. If we are more expensive than another company, chances are excellent that we are saving you money with experience, quality, and little extras that we do not charge you for separately.

Maintain your pool

Follow our instructions and recommendations. We are telling you these things to help you. Preventative maintenance now means less last minute emergency calls later. (Think Zinc Anodes if you have a salt pool – and if you don't have one, or don't know what it is, CALL US RIGHT NOW!)

Be a good customer

This means treating your service company and service techs with respect and understanding, especially when the season is very busy. Just imagine if you had 500 people calling you right now to fix the pool. You want to help everyone, but you have to prioritize.

Be patient

Again, we can't stress this enough. We want to be able to help you, as quickly as we can. Servicing pools is an art and those most qualified to do the best work are in the highest demand.

Plan your fixes

If you know something is coming up, make a call now to your service company and let them know what you would like to do. If it's a major project, we can help advise you when the best time to complete it will be, and let you know when we'll best be able to service your need.

Understand Seasonal Scheduling - Busy and Not as Busy Times

The pool season in Michigan, and in most mid-western areas, faces similar issues with the seasonal nature of the business. The pool season is hot from Mid April to Mid October, with the very busy times at opening (May) and closing (September). There are many qualified companies, ready to serve the needs of the area customers – sometimes the requests have to be delegated, prioritized, and planned, and that just might be why it took a pool company so long to get out to your pool.

Buying a House with a Pool

The fastest way to have a new pool is to buy a house that has one! If you do purchase a house with a pool, it is wise to hire an experienced pool professional, just like you hire a home inspector. Your professional can look over the pool and the equipment to give you an idea of the pool's condition. If the pool is unopened and/or neglected, their report is even more important. Most of the time, it is cheaper to fix a pool than to "fill it in", yet it can be an investment to "get a pool going again." As a seller, allowing your pool professional to talk with a potential buyer may be a good selling point, if you've been taking care of your pool. If they have been doing maintenance, they will be able to assure the buyer of the condition and, for first time pool owner, show them how easy it is to enjoy a pool.

202

---

[202] Southwestern themed vinyl liner pool with an auto cover built by Legendary Escapes

Pool Encyclopedia

Algae

Algae are microscopic plants which can change the appearance and color of your water.

They find their way into the pool through airborne spores, water, grass, moss and other matter.

Algae will absorb dissolved carbon dioxide and can cause pH to rise.

There are many species of algae, some are green, some are yellow also referred to mustard algae, black and pink algae.

They can be clinging or floating. The spores that produce algae are prevented when chlorine levels are maintained properly. Once algae takes hold, however, treatment becomes very necessary.

WARNING: DO NOT ALLOW SWIMMERS INTO A POOL HEAVILY POLLUTED WITH ALGAE - YOU MAY NOT SEE THEM IF THEY ARE IN DISTRESS AND SOME STRAINS OF ALGAE CAN BE TOXIC.

Algaecide

An "as-needed" chemical. If algae does occur, use an algaecide to kill the algae. Most algaecides are liquid. Once you determine the type of algae you have by color, you can add the appropriate algaecide, often in combination with pool shock. Always follow label directions.

If you have certain types of algae, especially mustard algae it will be advisable to also treat your pool equipment (brushes, hoses, vac heads and cleaners) to remove this persistent algae.

Green algae is the easiest to treat and remove, sometimes even just shocking the pool will take care of the issue.

Algistat

Algistats are used to help prevent algae, and can be used with other chemicals to help prevent algae outbreaks. Algistats are commonly sold as preventative or maintenance algaecides, and are commonly liquid.

Using an algistat as a preventative measure once per week during the season is highly advised.

Alkalinity Increaser

Alkalinity increaser is used to raise alkalinity in your swimming pool or spa. The scientific name is Sodium Bicarbonate. Sodium Bicarbonate is typically found labeled as "Alkalinity Increaser," "Alkalinity Up," or "Alkalinity Plus." Sodium Bicarbonate comes in a granular form.

Read the instructions on the label to determine the amount to add, how it must be added (either diluted in water or broadcast straight from the container), a maximum amount (per 10,000 gallons of water) that can be added at one time, and other precautions.

Automatic Vacuum Cleaners

An automatic vacuum cleaner is a vacuum that will be installed on either the suction or pressure side of your pool equipment system, or as a stand-alone addition to your pool. Refer to the section on automatic cleaners for further descriptions of each type.

Automatic Water Leveler

Evaporation and splash out are the main causes of water loss in a properly functioning pool. A water leveler will add water to the pool as the system determines the water level has dropped. There are simple levelers that will hang over the edge of the pool attached to a garden hose, or there are options that can be added into the equipment system.

Backwash Hose

A backwash hose is needed when there is a multi-port or push pull valve present to waste or backwash water from the swimming pool system. These are most common with sand filter and DE filter systems.

Some areas restrict the use of filters that require the backwash function. If you have a pool system with a cartridge filter it is unlikely you will have a backwash hose.

Backwash hoses are commonly blue flexible hose attached to the multiport, or it can be hard plumbed into a drain system or use pvc or flex pipe to send water away from your pool.

Bromine

Bromine is in the same halogen family as chlorine. It does have its advantages and disadvantages. Unlike chlorine, it cannot be stabilized with a product such as cyanuric acid. This is a problem with outdoor pools since the sun will quickly burn off the bromine. Bromine would need to be constantly added which would become costly. It is dosed into the pool by means of a circulatory feeder.

The main reason that bromine is *not* chosen as often as chlorine, is that it is fairly expensive. Bromine's niche is with spas (hot tubs), as it is more stable than chlorine in the hotter water temperatures.

Brush

Typically, a pool brush is 18" in length and has either nylon bristles or stainless steel bristles. Nylon bristles are safe for all pool types, stainless steel bristled brushes should only be used on gunite swimming pools.

Brushes are used to brush the pool walls and floor to remove debris, and algae.

Specialized brushes can come in many shapes and sizes.

The nylon bristle brush can be used with any type of pool to brush away dirt, debris, or Green & Mustard Algae. The stainless steel bristle brush can only be used on a concrete, gunite, shotcrete, or fiberglass pools to remove stubborn Black Algae, stubborn dirt, and any stains or scale. A stainless steel bristle brush can never be used with a vinyl-liner pool (it is too abrasive and may tear the liner).

Calcium Hardness

This is the amount of *dissolved* calcium (plus some other minerals like magnesium) in the water. Too much calcium in your water will cause cloudy water and scaling, which is a white chalky deposit that will form on pool surfaces, and inside equipment of pumps, heaters and salt cells.

Too little calcium in the water will contribute to water becoming aggressive and can etch and corrode the pool surface and metal components of the pool and equipment.

Calcium Hardness Increaser

Calcium Hardness Increaser is a chemical used to raise the hardness in a swimming pool or spa. It's scientific name is Calcium Chloride. You will find this commonly packaged and labeled as "Hardness Increaser," "Hardness Up," or "Hardness Plus."

Read the instructions on the label to determine the amount to add, how it should be added (either diluted in water or broadcast straight from the container), a maximum amount (per 10,000 gallons of water) that can be added at one time, and other precautions. Caution: adding calcium hardness increaser to water causes a reaction and water to become hot. Be careful not to mix in a container and touch the container, or touch the contents as a burn may occur.

Note: There is not a common product that is packaged and sold as a Hardness Decreaser, though there are some chemicals that will bind calcium in the water to lower levels that way. The best option, if your Hardness level is too high will be to drain some of your pool water and refill, and rebalance your chemical levels.

Calcium Hypochlorite

Calcium hypochlorite is a form of chlorine available that comes in granules or tablets. It is not stabilized, which means it will produce 65% available chlorine and be relatively fast acting. It tends to raise the pH.

Cement

A powdery substance made with calcined lime and clay. It is mixed with water to form mortar or mixed with sand, gravel, and water to make concrete, and is used as a building component in gunite swimming pools, as well as faux rocks and carved components, especially found in Legendary Escapes swimming pools.

Chlorine - Cl2

Chlorine is the most widely used chemical for swimming pool sanitizing. It kills bacteria through a chemical reaction which breaks down chlorine into hypochlorous acid and hypochlorite ions, which oxidize bacteria until they are either neutralized or destroyed.

Chlorine dissolves in water to form hypochlorus acid (HOCl or free chlorine - the principal water sanitizer) and hydrochloric acid.

Used at proper levels chlorine kills bacteria, living organisms, ammonia, and any other contaminates (such as dirt, debris, and algae spores) that are in pool water.

The two most common forms of chlorine used are granular chlorine (whose scientific name is "Dichlor") and chlorine tablets (whose scientific name is "Trichlor"). Chlorine tablets come in two sizes: 1" tablets and 3" tablets, as well as sticks.

Advantages of chlorine:

- ✓ It has a long half life, and can be stored in solid form for a long time.
- ✓ It comes in different forms
- ✓ It has a residual effect, and will neutralize contaminants when first added, and over time.

Concerns:

- ✓ Byproducts are chloramines and can cause skin and eye irritation

If you rely on chlorine for sanitizing your pool you should have a steady level of 1.0-3.0 ppm (parts per million) of chlorine in your pool.

You can add this in several ways. You can install an automatic chlorinator that takes tablets, either 1" or 3" that are added to your water as it flows through your system.

You can add liquid chlorine (which is the fastest acting version of chlorine, it is also the most quickly used up by your pool).

You can also add granular shock chlorine products to the pool, or in some cases use a floating chlorine dispenser. The rule of thumb for adding chlorine is 1 bag of shock or gallon per 10,000 gallons of pool water.

You can adjust and add more if the pool is green or cloudy. At openings we typically add 1 case (4 gallons) of liquid chlorine to all pools, and 2-3 cases for low water clarity, green, or in general really dirty/algae filled pools.

Another popular option is to install a chlorine generating cell/salt system to your pool. This uses regular salt, the cell converts the salt into the sodium and chlorine atoms, and the chlorine sanitizes your pool. It will then convert back into salt and maintain a healthy level in the pool until it is converted again, and helps to keep the pool clean.

Chlorine Alternatives

There are numerous chlorine alternatives on the market including bromine, Bacquacil, Revacil, (peroxide shock and polyhexamethylene[xx] Biguanide plastic polymer chain that will bind contaminants in the water and destroy them) mineral systems, chlorine generators (which produce chlorine from salts), iodine, and fluorine.

Over 90% of pool owners use chlorine or bromine (with the dominant percent still being chlorine).

The Pool Guy advises using chlorine or a salt generating system when possible. Individuals with sensitive skin or reason not to use chlorine are encouraged to look into alternative sanitizing systems.

Chlorine Demand

The amount of chlorine needed to destroy pollutants in pool water such as bacteria, algae and other contaminants.

Chlorine Donor

One of the many chlorine compounds available which, when dissolved in water, will provide chlorine or hypochlorus acid.

Chlorine Lock

Over time as stabilizer stabilizer (cyanuric acid) builds up in the water, it can attain levels that bind to chlorine and lock the chlorine. This makes it difficult for the dichlor or trichlor to react with the water and produce sufficient hypochlorus acid (free chlorine) to kill bacteria and other micro-organisms. This may happen in areas where pools are not drained and refilled for the winter/spring closing and opening cycles, and when stabilized chlorine is used, or an over abundance of cyanuric acid is added or present in water.

The solution to lowering the stabilizer levels is to drain and refill some of the pool water.

Chlorine Residual

The amount of chlorine left over after the chlorine demand has been met, it is what is left over after the chlorine has killed organic matter in the water.

Chlorine Stabilizer

The chemical name is cyanuric acid. It is also commonly referred to as stabilizer or conditioner.

It can be obtained as a granular product. It is also found in stabilized chlorine (and will be labeled as stabilized chlorine) often in dichlor or trichlor form. When stabilized forms of chlorine are mixed with water they dissociate (split up) into hypochlorus acid (free chlorine) and cyanuric acid (stabilizer).

Suggested levels of stabilizer are beneficial because they prevent wastage of free chlorine by the u/v waves in sunlight, but high levels are a disadvantage because they make it take longer for the chlorine to kill micro-organisms and can cause chlorine lock.

If you are using dichlor or trichlor, there should be no need to add extra stabilizer.

If you sanitize your pool with sodium hypochlorite or calcium hypochlorite which have no inbuilt stabilizer you will need to add some.

DANGER: do not mix these chemicals in the dry state.

Clarifier

An "as-needed" chemical used to clump smaller particles into larger clumps so the filter can remove them.

If you experience cloudy water it may be because of particulate in the water (bacteria, dirt, and other debris) that are suspended in the pool water. These particles are so small that the filter cannot trap them, unless they bind together in larger amounts.

Clarifiers are typically liquid, and the chemistry of what is in them is not often disclosed, other than it is typically a blend of polymers of some type. Clarifiers are often used with shock to restore water clarity.

Combined Chlorine Or Chloramines

When free chlorine reacts with nitrogen compounds which are introduced into pool water by swimmer pollution, combined chlorine or chloramines are formed which break down into ammonium compounds (hence, chlor + amine).

Combined chlorine and chloramines are ineffective as sanitizers, and nitrogen trichloride is the cause of the stale chlorine smell associated with public swimming pools.

Chloramines are broken down by raising the level of free chlorine through a shock process which will reach break point chlorination (enough free chlorine present to break the combined chlorine bonds.)

Cover Cleaner

Solar Cover Cleaner -

A cleaner used to clean off your solar cover.

To clean your solar cover, lay it out, spray it with a garden hose, and brush, use your cleaner and rinse.

NOTE: Take care when laying your cover on grass. The sun can quickly penetrate the cover and burn your grass.

Winter Cover Cleaner -

A cleaner used to clean off your winter cover. A garden hose and brush can be used with our without cover cleaner.

NOTE: Take care when laying your cover on grass. The sun can quickly penetrate the cover and burn your grass.

Cyanuric Acid

Cyanuric Acid, often referred to on the label as either "Conditioner" or "Stabilizer" will protect chlorine from being destroyed by the sun.

Chlorine in the form of free chlorine is susceptible to being destroyed by the ultraviolet rays of the sun. The cyanuric acid acts as an inner tube of sorts that chlorine can hang on to so when the sun hits it, it will stay in the water.

Some granular chlorine and all stabilized chlorine tablets contain Cyanuric Acid.

Cyanuric acid levels should be checked periodically throughout the season and adjusted as needed. Cyanuric acid often takes a long time to dissolve, should be added gradually, and will increase filter pressure and should not be backwashed for at least 48 hours.

Cyanuric Acid is NOT used with Bromine or any other of the alternatives to chlorine.

DE

DE or diatomaceous earth is an effective filter media made up of fossilized diatoms which are porous microscopic sponge like organisms. DE coats the grids inside of a DE filter and traps particles, which will then be dislodged when the filter is backwashed and cleaned, and a new coating of DE will be applied.

Defoamer

Defoamer is liquid that can be sued to eliminate foam from pool or spa water. It is most commonly used in spas. Foam is caused by total dissolved solids, a byproduct of chemicals used, and body oils, lotions and shampoo or detergent products.

Dichlor

Dichlor is short for the chemical name of sodium dichloroisocyanurate dihydrate.

This is one of the stabilized chlorine donors (trichlor is the other.) It is called dichlor because there are two atoms of chlorine bonded to nitrogen on the molecule (sodium is bonded to the third nitrogen) trichlor has three.

Dichlor is usually packaged in granular form with 55% available chlorine.

When dissolved in water, it dissociates (splits up) into hypochlorous acid (free chlorine) and cyanuric acid.

Enzyme Cleaner

Enzyme cleaners are liquid form and can be used to breakdown and eliminate the dirty water line (also called the water ring or scum ring) that often forms around the top edge of swimming pools on the tile line, from fluctuations in the water level.

Products such as suntan lotions, underarm deodorants, and women's make-up, as well as body oils & dirt, can attach to the pool walls (just above the surface of the water) to cause this water line.

The Enzyme cleaner will react with the contaminants and break them down into liquid form to eliminate this water line.

Read the instructions on the label to determine the amount to add, how it should be added (most manufacturers of Enzyme cleaners recommend pouring it straight from the bottle), and other precautions.

Foam will often appear immediately after adding an enzyme cleaner. This signals the enzymes are reacting with the water line contaminants.

FerriTabs

Ferri-Iron Tabs are swimming pool water treatment tablets that help eliminate the discoloration caused by iron and manganese. They have been formulated for use in all filters (see package labels).

These double-action tablets are formulated to help decolorize water that has been colored by IRON or MANGANESE. These discoloring insoluble materials are removed from the water by charge neutralization and flocculation.

This non-toxic formulation is completely soluble in water and contains no caustic or corrosive chemicals, diatomaceous earth, alum, or any chemicals that will alter the pH or chlorine level of the water.

Make sure pool water has a pH of 7.2-7.6, and contains a measurable amount of chlorine by adjusting with chemicals as necessary. Chlorine will not affect the Ferri-Iron Tab action on Iron or Manganese. Make sure the pool filter is in good operating condition and has been turned on.

Drop 1 tablet for each 3000 gallons of pool water into the skimmer basket. In large pools that have multiple skimmers distribute the tablets.

For best results, add the required tablets over a period of a few hours, while the filter is operating. In order to permanently improve the water quality, the filter must be thoroughly back-washed within 18-24 hours after treatment.

In pools that have severe problems, repeat dosage and back-wash procedures after 24-48 hours.

In order to prevent a recurrence, when adding make up water, add 1 tablet for each 3000 gallons or less of fresh water.

Ferri-Iron Tabs can be shipped anywhere in the United States and most other countries.

Filter Cleaner

Filter Cleaners do not have a direct effect on water chemistry. They clean the filter, which does have a direct effect on water chemistry.

Filter Cleaners can be liquid or granular.

Purchase the specified Filter Cleaner for your type of filter.

Note: since Filter Cleaners are less of a chemical and more of a cleaner, it is okay to pour a Filter Cleaner in the skimmer. *It is NEVER recommended to pour or place any chemical in the skimmer.*

Garden Hose Operated Vacuum

Some pools do not have suction lines in order to vacuum the pool with a manual vacuum assembly and so a garden hose operated vacuum is used.

There are two types of vacuum units: the brush-style vacuum unit and the wheel-style vacuum unit.

The brush-style vacuum unit is used for vinyl-liner pools. The wheel-style vacuum unit is used for concrete, gunite, shotcrete, and fiberglass pools.

Your standard garden hose will attach to the vacuum unit. The running water from your garden hose will create suction, drawing the leaves, dirt, and other debris into the silt bag of the vacuum unit. Once full, empty the silt bag, reattach it to the vacuum unit, and start again until the silt bag is full, etc. until you're done.

Many pool owners with the capability to use a manual vacuum assembly will also have a hose operated vacuum.

If there is an enormous amount of leaves and other large debris on the pool floor it may be too much to net out or manually vacuum.

[203]*Gunite*

Before we get into that, the photo above is of a gunite pool in Highland, MI built by Legendary Escapes. The pool was formed, and then shot in gunite, as was the base for the waterfall that you see in the background. The gunite

surface was then finished with pebble. Sometimes a white marcite coating, pebble, or quartz will be used to seal the gunite surface.

[204]Shotcrete is concrete (or sometimes mortar) conveyed

through a hose and pneumatically projected at high velocity onto a surface, as a construction technique.

Shotcrete is usually an all-inclusive term; gunite is a term sometimes used for some dry-mix types.

Shotcrete undergoes placement and compaction at the same time due to the force with which it is projected from the nozzle. It can be impacted onto any type or shape of surface, including vertical or overhead areas.

Shotcrete, then known as gunite, was invented in the early 1900s by American taxidermist Carl Akeley, used to fill plaster model of animals. He used the method of blowing dry material out of a hose with compressed air, injecting water at the nozzle

---

[203]Gunite pool, rough construction
[204] Gunite pool built by Legendary Escapes Pools

as it was released. This was later used to patch weak parts in old buildings. In 1911, he was granted a patent for his inventions, the "cement gun", the equipment used, and "gunite", the material that was produced. Until the 1950s when the wet-mix process was devised, only the dry-mix process was used. In the 1960s, the alternative method for gunning by the dry method was devised with the development of the rotary gun, with an open hopper that could be fed continuously. Shotcrete is also a viable means and method for placing structural concrete.

Shotcrete is today an all-inclusive term that describes spraying concrete or mortar with either a dry or wet mix process. However, it may also sometimes be used to distinguish from gunite as a wet-mix. The term shotcrete was first defined by the American Railway Engineers Association (AREA) in the early 1930s.[1] By 1951, shotcrete had become the official generic name of the sprayed concrete process.[1]

Gunite refers only to the dry-mix process, in which the dry cementitious mixture is blown through a hose to the nozzle, where water is injected immediately before application. Gunite was the original term coined by Akeley, trademarked in 1909 and patented in North Carolina. The concrete is blasted by pneumatic pressure from a gun, hence "gun"-ite.

The term "Gunite" became the registered trademark of Allentown, the oldest manufacturer of gunite equipment. Other manufacturers were thus compelled to use other terminology to describe the process such as shotcrete, pneumatic concrete, guncrete, etc. Shotcrete emerged as the most commonly used term other than gunite, and after the later development of the wet process came to be used for both methods.

And that is what you need to know about gunite, shotcrete and concrete.

Hard Water

Water is considered hard if its calcium hardness is over 250 ppm and its alkalinity is over 150 ppm.

Hybrid Swimming Pool (TM)

A Hybrid Swimming Pool (TM) is a combination of the elements of a gunite pool with a vinyl liner pool, developed by Allan Curtis of Legendary Escapes in the Michigan market.

It can be described as a pool with a basin created using both technologies of vinyl liner and gunite. Vinyl is comfortable for swimmers and gunite allows the designer freedom with shapes, sills, slides, waterfalls, grottos, swim-up bars/tables, ceramic tile lines and more. Where vinyl meets gunite is where the magic of this dual personality pool comes together. The final look is seamless.

The building of hybrid swimming pools has been pioneered by Al Curtis {Ask the Pool Guy} of Legendary Escapes. Curtis has revolutionized the swimming pool industry with this new design and construction technique, resulting in artistic and creative combination pools.

205

Hypobromous Acid (Free Bromine)

Hypobromous acid or free bromine is the main disinfectant in pools on bromine or BCDMH. It is formed (a) by dissociation when BCDMH is dissolved in water and (b) by the reaction between hypochlorus acid and spent bromine (bromide ion). It is commonly used in spas and hot tubs as it is effective over a much wider range of pH values and at higher temperatures.

Hypochlorite Ion (OCl)

The is chlorine resulting from dissociation (splitting up) of hypochlorus acid (HOCl) into its constituent parts - H+ and OCl- (hypochlorite ion).

This will happen if the pH of the water is high.

If the pH is too low the hypochlorus acid dissociates into molecular chlorine (CL2).

---

[205] Hybrid Swimming Pool built by Legendary Escapes

The hypochlorite ion is a poor disinfectant because the negative charge creates an obstacle to penetrating the wall of the cell. Hypochlorus acid is 100 times faster than hypochlorite ion in killing a micro-organism.

Hypochlorus Acid - HOCl

Also known as free chlorine, it is formed when calcium hypochlorite, dichlor, trichlor or chlorine gas are mixed with water and dissociate. This is the main pool water disinfectant.

Hypochlorus acid acts (a) as a sanitizer killing potentially harmful bacteria and micro-organisms (it can enter a cell's wall and upset its protein and enzyme function), (b) as an oxidizing agent eliminating organic and inorganic impurities by a process similar to combustion e.g. it burns out pollution introduced by swimmers such as sweat and urine (yes, I'm afraid people do).

Useful amounts of hypochlorus acid can only be obtained if the pH is within certain limits or if the stabilizer level is not too high.

Ionization

Ionization is the process in which a current is supplied to a sacrificial electrode made of various metals and subatomic particles ions are pulled off and pass through a stream of running water which neutralize disease causing organisms.

The metals can be copper, copper/silver, or copper/zinc.

These metals are toxic to many types of bacteria and algae. Pool ionization is not a stand-alone sanitizer and additional sanitizing, often by chlorine is needed.

In-Floor Cleaning System/In-Floor Heating & Efficiency

In-Floor cleaning systems have low profile fixtures that pop-up automatically (driven by the system) to move debris to the drain and out of the pool. They also are more efficient for heating the pool, as the jets are located on the bottom of the pool resulting in heating from the bottom up.

Langelier Saturation Index

Langelier Saturation Index (LSI) is a calculation for a pool or spa. The LSI assesses the overall balance of the water. If you are interested, you can find an online source for "Langelier Saturation Index Calculator." Enter your readings and you can determine whether your water is corrosive, balanced or scale-forming. Note: you must enter all parameters to calculate this index correctly.

Manual Vacuum Assembly

This typically consists of a vac head for your pool type, the vacuum hose, the vacpole, and perhaps a vacuum seal plate for the skimmer.

There are two styles of vac heads: the brush-style vac head, often triangular in shape for use in a vinyl liner pool, and the wheel-style vac head, typically rectangular in shape for use in gunite and fiberglass pools.

One end of the vacuum hose connects to the vac head (the end that swivels) and the other to your skimmer. Do not mix these up, as you may introduce air into your system if the end that swivels is in the skimmer and prevent the system from priming properly.

If needed a vacuum seal plate should be placed over the skimmer in order to trap debris in the skimmer basket, and for the best suction.

Some pools are built with a designated vacuum line for the end of the vac hose.

Use your telescoping vacpole to maneuver the vacuum assembly across the pool floor and walls.

Metal Sequestering Agent

Metal Sequestering Agents can either be liquid or granular and are used to treat odd tints to the color of the pool water, stains, or the formation of scale. These colors and stains may result from the minerals that are present in the tap water that is used to fill the pool (such as copper, iron, manganese, magnesium, or calcium) or from poor water chemistry and leeching from pool equipment and surfaces.

If an odd tint, any stains, or the formation of scale are present, the condition can often be remedied by correcting and maintaining proper water chemistry and by using a Metal Sequestering Agent, which will rid the water of these excess minerals.

Read the instructions on the label to determine the amount to add, how it should be added (either diluted in water or poured/broadcast straight from the bottle/container), and other precautions.

Muriatic Acid

Muriatic Acid can be used to lower pH and Alkalinity, as well as for cleaning tile and gunite pool surfaces. It can be added directly to swimming pool water, and poured directly on tile and gunite surfaces to release surface staining. It is also used during acid washes, with a metal bristled brush to etch the surface of gunite, pebble and marcite to release surface stains.

Muriatic acid is in liquid form. Some forms are sold with additives to reduce the odor and accidental exposure to the elements which cause irritation.

NOTE: Be extra careful when handling muriatic acid. It is highly corrosive and can react chemically with normal clothing. The fumes are also dangerous and can damage your respiratory tract and linings of your organs, wearing a mask for fume inhalation prevention is advised, as well as gloves and safety goggles.

299

Nets

There are two styles of standard pool nets:

The deep net, which is often called a leaf rake, has a wide opening and a bag shaped net. This style of net is primarily used to reach leaves or other large debris that have settled to the pool floor. The deep net can also be used to skim leaves and debris off the surface of the water, but the skimmer net is best at performing this task.

The skimmer net, which has a shallow net, is primarily used to remove leaves, grass clippings, debris, or insects that float on the surface of the water.

Ozone

Ozone generators are found in many commercial swimming pool systems, as an additional treatment for water. They ozonate water in pipes, and no ozone enters the pool. Ozone is a gas that is produced by ultraviolet light exposure to oxygen. It is injected into water, and will kill bacteria present.

Ozone is not an alternative to chlorine or the primary sanitizing method in a pool. It is meant to supplement as an additional treatment.

Ozone is most common in spas and hot tubs, and works effectively with both chlorine and bromine sanitizers.

Ozone kills bacteria and certain organisms which can cause illness, more effectively than chlorine. It also prevent airborne endotoxins, as well as oxidize and destroys oils and other water contaminants.

Ozone is pH neutral and adds no contaminants into water.

Parts Per Million (ppm)

Equivalent to milligrams per liter (mg/l). The standard way of quantifying the amount of chemicals or minerals in the water.

For an idea of scale, 1 ppm is equal to 1 milligram per liter. So, 5 ppm is 5 milligrams for every liter of water. Or a 5/1,000,000 ratio.

pH

pH is the measurement of acidity of water and measured on a scale of 0 to 14 with 7 being neutral (water).

A pH below 7.0 means the water is very acidic, as the pH approaches 8.0, the water becomes very basic (alkaline).

Proper pH levels allow the other chemicals to work properly, and keep an optimal balance in water chemistry. Low or high levels can cause damage to a vinyl liner.

Under the right circumstances, with pH below 7.0, the liner can actually grow and develop unsightly wrinkles. We refer to those as pH wrinkles. There is no way to remove them besides installing a new liner. High pH greatly accelerates the aging process and shortens the life of the liner, and will often cause cloudy water and surface scaling.

Chlorine is less effective at higher pH levels. At a pH of 8.0; chlorine is only 22% effective.

Use pH+ or pH- to adjust the pH of your water. Always address the Total Alkalinity level first as it can cause the pH level to fluctuate.

pH Decreaser

Used to lower pH and Alkalinity. The scientific name is Sodium Bisulfate and is typically packaged and sold as "pH Decreaser," pH Down," or "pH Minus."

Sodium Bisulfate is granular and is commonly referred to as "dry acid" (as opposed to the liquid Muriatic Acid, which is an alternative to lowering pH and Alkalinity).

Note: Sodium Bisulfate is also used to lower Alkalinity. *There is no product that is packaged as an "Alkalinity Decreaser."*

pH Increaser

Used to raise pH. The Scientific name is Sodium Carbonate and is typically packaged and sold as "pH Increaser," "pH Up," or "pH Plus." Sodium Carbonate is granular.

Pool Filtration System (Example)

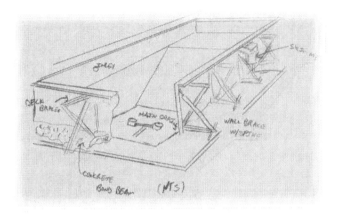

Pool Filtration Diagram

ppm

See: Parts Per Million.

Salt System or Chlorine Generator or Generating System

Salt generating systems use salt added to pool water, run through a chlorine generators which break the salt into sodium and chlorine.

The chlorine cleans your pool and clears the water; then, when the chlorine has done its job, it hooks back up with the sodium and turns back into salt.

The salt is recycled continuously, day after day and this system provides a continual release of the chlorine sanitizing agent into your water.

Note: A salt water pool will conduct trace amounts of electricity, resulting in electrolysis potential in your pool. A zinc anode protects the metal components of your swimming pool from corrosion. The zinc anode will be the first thing to corrode, saving the other parts of your pool from corrosion. If you have a salt pool make sure you have a zinc anode. *They are often overlooked, and are a critical part of your system!*

Shock

Shock is often referred to as the act of shocking a pool, and the substance used to superchlorinate or shock and oxidize a pool. Shocking a pool should happen at least once per week, and as needed during the pool season.

Shock can come in a granular form in both chlorine and non chlorine forms, and is also often used as a term for liquid chlorine.

If you use chlorine to chlorinate your pool you will want to predominantly use a chlorine-based shock (such as Calcium Hypochlorite or Lithium Hypochlorite).

If you use an alternative to chlorine sanitizing such as a non-chlorinating method like Baquacil or Revacil, you need to use their specific shock products.

If you use bromine, you will want to predominantly use a non-chlorine shock (such as Potassium Peroxymonosulfate). You can supplement your shock schedule with a chlorine-based shock periodically.

No, neither a 1910 bathing costume or tiny polka-dot bikini will shock your pool.

Shock Chlorine

Usually a short-hand way of referring to sodium hypochlorite or calcium hypochlorite, which can be dosed into the pool at a high rate, without increasing levels of stabilizer (cyanuric acid).

The purpose of shock dosing is to achieve breakpoint chlorination, and to increase the amount of free available chlorine to combined chlorine or chloramines in your pool.

It can also be used as treatment for a problem such as algae growth, cloudy water or unpleasant chlorine smells.

It does this by satisfying chlorine demand i.e. by killing bacteria, algae, and other micro-organisms, and breaking down accumulated organic impurities to leave a chlorine residual.

Shotcrete

See Gunite

Soda Ash

An alternative to raise pH. Like Sodium Carbonate (pH Increaser), Soda Ash is also granular.

Soft Water

Water is considered soft if has a hardness of under 50 ppm as calcium carbonate and an alkalinity of under 30 ppm as calcium chloride. The pH can be rather unstable in soft water areas, but alkaline chlorine donors such as calcium hypochlorite will help to increase hardness as will the addition of calcium chloride.

Superchlorination

Superchlorination is often interchanged with the term shock or shocking a pool.

Superchlorination is commonly used to raise chlorine levels to around 10 ppm to *prevent* bacteria or algae infestation and can be used to reach breakpoint chlorination.

Testing - Testing Kits and Routines

You must constantly test for chlorine (or its alternative), pH, and Alkalinity at the poolside.

Approximately once per month, or if unusual pool readings occur, take a water sample to your local pool professionals and have them test every chemical reading on the computer.

Test chlorine (or its alternative), as well as pH and Alkalinity, 2 - 3 times per week during normal weather conditions and under normal use.

Test chlorine (or its alternative) daily during periods of scorching temperatures, unbearable humidity, and intense sunlight, as well as times when swimmer load is at its highest.

Test chlorine (or its alternative), as well as pH and Alkalinity, after heavy rainfall, before and after a pool party, and, of course, if water appears to be cloudy, murky, or beginning to form algae.

The only way that you can accurately determine your water chemistry is by testing. You cannot count on a visual test to indicate the appropriate levels.

Tile & Vinyl Cleaner

A cleaner to clean the walls (and tiles, if applicable) of concrete, gunite, shotcrete, or fiberglass pools, and to clean liners of vinyl-liner pools.

This product is fairly effective for eliminating light dirt, discolorations or stains. The product is safe to mix with your pool water when used with manufacturer instructions.

Total Alkalinity

Closely related to pH, it is the first chemical to adjust, prior to making a pH adjustment as it buffers the pH changes in the water.

Total alkalinity is a measure of the amount of alkaline materials in the water. This alkalinity will usually be present as bicarbonates, but with a very high pH carbonates and hydroxides can be present as well.

Alkalinity is a measuring of the alkaline materials dissolved in water. With the alkalinity in the range of 100 to 150 ppm, it helps pH to resist fluctuations. If the alkalinity is low the result is that the "pH will bounce" in and out of range.

The relevance to pH is that the amount of alkali (hardness) in the water will determine how easy it is for changes in pH to occur.

If the alkalinity is too low (below 80 ppm) there can be rapid fluctuations in pH - i.e. there is insufficient 'buffer' to the pH. High alkalinity (above 200 ppm) will result in the water being too buffered - it will make it difficult to adjust or correct the pH.

Pools with an alkalinity problem often coupled with a pH problem will see issues with the heater core. When these are out of balance water becomes aggressive, and will corrode the inside of your heater core (which contains copper – so if you have copper in your water and have no other source, it's most likely from your heater). If this happens, you want to remedy your water balance problem quickly and you may need to replace your heater core, or in some cases, the entire heater.

High alkalinity and high pH can lead to cloudy water and scale formation. Low alkalinity can result in corrosion and discomfort to swimmers.

Total Chlorine

Free chlorine plus combined chlorine. Hence chloramine levels can be worked out by the formula: Combined chlorine = total chlorine (from DPD no 3 tablet) - free chlorine (DPD no 1 tablet).

Total Dissolved Solids (TDS)

As a measurement of the total amount of matter (minerals, chemical residue, dust, dirt, and other particles) that are dissolved in water.

Water can only absorb so many components. When TDS becomes too high, the water cannot absorb chemicals, and will render them ineffective.

The best way to control TDS is backwashing and refreshing of water in a swimming pool. In southern states where pools are not drained and refilled during opening and closing times, the TDS may become out of balance. Evaporation will also allow solids left behind to add up in the balance of the water.

The highest level of TDS for a pool is 1,500 ppm. However, salt systems will need to measured considering the salt ppm separately from the TDS measurement.

At values above 1500 ppm we begin to notice stains in the pool. It will also reduce the activity of any chemicals you add, preventing them from doing what they're supposed to. The water may also become cloudy.

As water evaporates, only the water itself evaporates. Minerals, chemical residue, and other particles are left behind and remain in the pool water. With evaporation, you need to continually add water. As you add tap water up to the standard operating water level (half way up the skimmer), you are also adding additional minerals and particles. Although these minerals and other particles from tap water do add to the TDS reading, it is extremely minimal.

The biggest factor is that this new tap water will soon be introduced to chemicals. It is the chemical residue that is not filtered and remains in the pool water that has the greatest effect on increasing TDS. Whenever chemicals are added, the TDS reading will increase.

Eventually, this matter that remains in the pool water will act as a sponge, consuming your new chemicals, rendering them virtually ineffective. It will take many years (approximately 6-8 years) for the TDS reading to become so high that it will consume your chemicals before they can engage in their intended purpose. (6-8 years is a guideline only.)

There is no chemical that can lower the TDS reading into an ideal range. Rather, a TDS reading can only be lowered by draining your pool, either partially or completely, and adding fresh water.

If it has been some time since your pool was last drained and cleaned, there are certain indicators that may tell you that your TDS reading is contributing to water balance issues:

> Continual addition of excess chemicals.
> Water chemistry tests fine, but water is still not clean, clear, blue and sparkling.
> Various water chemistry problems include:
> Colored yet clear water (the water has an odd tint, but you can still see the pool floor).
> Algae growth despite a good chlorine (or its alternative) reading and proper overall water chemistry (pH and Alkalinity).
> Varying and false readings on chemical tests.

If any of these are the case with your pool, or if other water chemistry issues are present, we suggest you have your TDS tested and correct the issue appropriately.

In a salt pool, where the salt is dissolved in the water and is set to run at between 3500 ppm and 4000 ppm, the salt concentration needs to be omitted from the TDS measurement.

Trichlor

Short for *trichlor*oisocyanuric acid - a bit easier to say than the chemical name for dichlor. This is a stabilized chlorine donor. It is called trichlor because there are three atoms of chlorine bonded to the nitrogen on the molecule. This makes it stronger than dichlor which only has two.

Usually sold in the form of slow dissolving tablets of 91% available chlorine. When dissolved in water, trichlor dissociates (splits up) into free chlorine and cyanuric acid.

UV Ozone Generators

UV Ozone generators use Mercury to create Ozone, and are commonly used as secondary systems in commercial pools and in hot tubs and spas. Ozone is a powerful oxidizer, it neutralizes contaminants in swimming pools by releasing oxygen atoms which combine with algae, bacteria and oils to change or destroy them. Ozone has no effect on pH levels of swimming pools. An ozone generator can only be used as a secondary system, and a main sanitizing method must be used.

Vacpole

A long aluminum pole that can extend to various lengths in order reach all areas of the pool.

It is a multi-function tool that will attach to nets, brushes, vacuum heads, and other maintenance equipment. It will also attach to the "Shepherd's Crook," which is a life-hook (a life-saving device).

Water Balance

Water balance is the balance of the chemical makeup of water.

All water, tap water, bottled water, and pool water have minerals in them. Your pool needs a specific balance to be safe and balanced.

Zinc Anode

A zinc anode is a critical part of your salt water swimming pool system. It becomes the sacrificial metal for trace electrical charges in the water and was designed to stop metal erosion and plaster discoloration due to galvanic corrosion. There are many options for zinc anodes including skimmer discs, ladder and light bolt on options, and anodes to be plumbed in at the equipment pad.

Zoo

Consider posting your pool rules and enforce them or you will have one, a Zoo that is. Here are some things to consider:

- ➤ No sharp objects in and around the pool.
- ➤ No glass containers in the pool area. Broken glass is very hard to see in the water and will cut your vinyl liner, if you have one, as well as swimmers.
- ➤ No diving – unless your pool was designed for it.
- ➤ No pushing – not everyone can swim and they may hit something harder than their head.
- ➤ Children should take frequent toilet breaks and clean up well. Wash hands. (Really.)
- ➤ Swimming Babies – It's never too early to learn – yet even a small amount of fecal matter can make another swimmer sick. Be sure the child is clean before entering the pool. Everybody out, if there is an incident. (Note: Swim Diapers are no guarantee of containment.) Also, change diapers in a bathroom or a diaper-changing area and not at poolside.
- ➤ No swimming for someone who is sick, especially when they have diarrhea. They can spread germs in the water and make other people sick.
- ➤ (Ladies, it's fine with internal protection.)
- ➤ Swimsuit required? (Please consider your neighbors.)

- ➤ Bathing Cap required?
- ➤ No swimming alone?
- ➤ Noise level limit? (Please be kind to neighbors.)
- ➤ No running?
- ➤ No splashing?
- ➤ Ah yes! Have fun!

You are the final authority. It's your pool!

Happy Swimming!

About the Authors

Allan Curtis, Sandi Maki

A founder who is part pool builder, part artist and part philosopher, with a dream of creating backyard experiences that are one-of-a-kind. A managing partner who isn't afraid to question everything to come up with a better way to work, play and live. A crew that is encouraged to pour nothing but good energy into everything they touch. Plus a healthy dose of think-outside-the-box marketing and inspirational thought leadership. That's the magic behind the team of Ask the Pool Guy, a service company based in Southeastern Michigan, and their partner company, Legendary Escapes, a boutique hybrid pool building company in southeast Michigan.

Originally a vinyl pool building and service company, Al Curtis and Sandi Maki have grown Ask the Pool Guy into a sought after service company in the Southeastern Michigan Market, using that as a guide to launch a national service franchise.

They have also built Legendary Escapes into a sought-after premium pool building company by relentlessly striving to refine the work they do, who they do it for, and how they go about it. In the process, they have also created a business support group (aka the Insights Clubhouse) where small business owners gather to share innovative thinking on creating businesses and lives in which they can truly express their passions and their Certain Way.

Al and Sandi are both published authors, social media leaders and sought-after public speakers who are always willing to listen, learn, share and grow.

Their enthusiasm is infectious, and their work speaks for itself.

Allan Curtis & Sandi Maki,
Ask the Pool Guy & Ask the Pool Girl

End Note Resources

i Sinek, Simon. *Start with Why: How Great Leaders Inspire Everyone to Take Action*. New York: Portfolio, 2009. Print.

ii www.FerriIronTabs.com

iii "AquaBRIGHT." *EcoFINISH*. N.p., n.d. Web. 24 Feb. 2016.

iv LathamPool.com

v http://www.aquachek.com/

vi https://www.youtube.com/user/askthepoolguy

vii http://www.pentairpool.com/products/automation-easytouch-control-systems-49.htm

viii http://www.pentairpool.com/products/automation-screenlogic2-interface-for-intellitouch-and-easytouch-automation-systems-418.htm

ix http://www.maytronics.com/robotic-pool-cleaners

x Pool Center. (n.d.). Retrieved from http://poolcenter.com

xi Ribar, Matthew. "Non Chlorine Shock vs. Chlorinated Shock in Swimming Pools. Ask the Pool Guy. (n.d.). Retrieved from http://askthepoolguy.com

xii http://www.halosource.com/Products/SeaKlear/SeaKlear-SDS-List.aspx

xiii http://www.pentairpool.com/support/calculators/pool-pump-calc/index.htm

xiv http://www.bluesquaremfg.com/

xv https://www.hayward-pool.com/

xvi https://en.wikipedia.org/wiki/Biofilm

xvii www.naturallyjodi.com

xviii Traylor, Nate. "Battle of the Bulge." *PoolSpaNews*. N.p., 16 Mar. 2015. Web. 25 Feb. 2016.

xix http://www.ecopoolfinish.com/

xx Romanowski, Eric G., Kathleen A. Yates, Katherine E. O'Connor, Francis S. Mah, Robert M. Q. Shanks, and Regis P. Kowalski. "The Evaluation of Polyhexamethylene Biguanide (PHMB) as a Disinfectant for Adenovirus." *JAMA Ophthalmology*. U.S. National Library of Medicine, n.d. Web. 03 Mar. 2016.

59635505R00173

Made in the USA
Charleston, SC
11 August 2016